Cambridge Elements ≡

Elements in Evolutionary Economics
edited by
John Foster
University of Queensland
Jason Potts
RMIT University

COEVOLUTION IN ECONOMIC SYSTEMS

Isabel Almudi

University of Zaragoza

Francisco Fatas-Villafranca

University of Zaragoza

CAMBRIDGE
UNIVERSITY PRESS

University Printing House, Cambridge CB2 8BS, United Kingdom

One Liberty Plaza, 20th Floor, New York, NY 10006, USA

477 Williamstown Road, Port Melbourne, VIC 3207, Australia

314–321, 3rd Floor, Plot 3, Splendor Forum, Jasola District Centre,
New Delhi – 110025, India

79 Anson Road, #06–04/06, Singapore 079906

Cambridge University Press is part of the University of Cambridge.

It furthers the University's mission by disseminating knowledge in the pursuit of
education, learning, and research at the highest international levels of excellence.

www.cambridge.org
Information on this title: www.cambridge.org/9781108737999
DOI: 10.1017/9781108767798

First published 2021

A catalogue record for this publication is available from the British Library.

ISBN 978-1-108-73799-9 Paperback
ISSN 2514-3573 (online)
ISSN 2514-3581 (print)

Coevolution in Economic Systems

Elements in Evolutionary Economics

DOI: 10.1017/9781108767798
First published online: May 2021

Isabel Almudi
University of Zaragoza

Francisco Fatas-Villafranca
University of Zaragoza

Author for correspondence: Isabel Almudi, ialmudi@unizar.es

Abstract: Coevolution in economic systems plays a key role in the dynamics of contemporary societies. Coevolution operates when, considering several evolving realms within a socioeconomic system, these realms mutually shape their respective innovation, replication and/or selection processes. The processes that emerge from coevolution should be analyzed as being globally codetermined in dynamic terms. The notion of coevolution appears in the literature on modern innovation economics since the neo-Schumpeterian inception four decades ago. In this Element, these antecedents are drawn on to formally clarify and develop how the coevolution notion can expand the analytical and methodological scope of evolutionary economics, allowing for further unification and advance of evolutionary subfields.

Keywords: coevolution, evolutionary modeling, Schumpeterian economics, innovation, evolutionary political economy

JEL classifications: B52, C63, O31, O57, P16

ISBNs: 9781108737999 (PB), 9781108767798 (OC)
ISSNs: 2514-3573 (online), 2514-3581 (print)

Contents

1 Introduction

In this Element, we define *coevolution* in economic systems as a force operating among interactive realms, in such a way that the respective innovation, replication and selection domain-specific mechanisms become dynamically codetermined across domains. Our perspective draws on the idea that reality is a plural composition of domains that, despite being to some extent self-referential, are transversally connected in a dynamic manner. We present and extend these ideas as a development of previous contributions within the realm of evolutionary economics.

Thus, we claim and try to show that the coevolution perspective may expand the analytical scope of evolutionary economics. For instance, we state that coevolution can help to close the gaps between the innovation systems approach and the realm of Schumpeterian industrial dynamics; it can unify methodologies for evolutionary theorizing (agent-based models (ABMs), population dynamics modeling); and it can shed new light on such issues as the emergence of market order and price formation in innovative economies, the imperfection of selection mechanisms observed in industrial dynamics, the co-development of practice and understanding driving growth and sustainable technological advance, as well as the potential outcomes from the competition of ideologies in contemporary evolving democracies. Before we move on to the specific complementary frames in which we explore these processes, in Section 2 we define key concepts and delineate our methodological approach.

In Section 3, we propose a coevolutionary two-sector approach to the analysis of price formation in innovative multisector settings. We show how the innovative capacity of an upstream-production sector can be constrained by the absorptive capacity of the downstream-user sector and we study the fundamentals of price dynamics and market orders that emerge. We obtain explanations (resting on coevolution) for the well-known empirical finding that competition in real markets seems to be imperfect, in the sense that real selection processes do not validate the evolutionary prediction of the selection of the fittest. Likewise, since coevolution points to a new type of coordination problem resting on the unbalanced knowledge evolution of multisectoral economies, we pose a new role for innovation policy to create sectorally targeted balancing actions. The model is explored through a combination of closed-form techniques and computational experiments.

Following this, and drawing on Sections 2 and 3, we devote Section 4 to developing the argument that technological progress emerges from the coevolution between bodies of practice and understanding. We formally explore consequences of the existence of mutually dependent selection processes at work in both realms, and we extract implications regarding catalysts of coevolution and blocking factors. We then pick out these factors and study the engines of economic growth in a new multisectoral setting. The coevolution between firms, industrial structures, technological advances and supporting institutions underlying growth is formally analyzed. The exploration of this proposal leads us to obtain a statistical index (the $\mathcal{T}$–index), which may be relevant for science and technology policy as well as for tackling sustainability issues. We close Section 4 by reflecting on certain political economy implications of possible growth scenarios in the near future. Clearly, there are some urgent issues that have arisen from the contemporary Covid-19 pandemic, the great lockdown in 2020 and the unfreezing of the economy and these are discussed in this section.

Section 5 takes up the political economy concerns that arise from Section 4. Thus, we propose a coevolutionary representation of socioeconomic orders as resulting from competing subsystems of citizen-envisioned worldviews, in such a way that citizens seek to affect the relative balance of public opinion and its materialization in institutional power structures in order to advance toward their envisioned organization of society. They do so by contributing ideas and resources to competing ideological/institutional settings. The combination of formal and computational analysis allows us to analyze the role of behavioral diversity, the feedbacks from global dynamics to individual perceptions and initial configurations in the coevolution of worldviews and social structures.

Apart from the theoretical and policy results that are obtained in this work, we look for and back the methodological strategy that we believe is the most fruitful for the development of evolutionary economics – namely, the systematic use of formal theorizing grounded in evolutionary microfoundations and represented in low-scale models, with these models being amenable to the analytical combination of computational methods and closed-form mathematical tools. Once we come up with coevolution models of this type, not only will new properties emerge but also fresh policy recommendations on crucial contemporary issues will arise. Certain potential lines for the development of this perspective in future works are synthesized in Section 6. The Appendices develop some of the technicalities necessarily involved in our coevolution approach.

2 Coevolution: A Key Concept for Evolutionary Economics

The main statement of this Element is that the idea of *coevolution* can play a key organizing role in evolutionary economic theory. From ontological and heuristic perspectives, the coevolution principle opens up new ways for constructing a general coherent framework in evolutionary economics. From methodological and theoretical viewpoints, it provides a way to work out new models to deal with open issues in economic theory.

We can find references to the notion of coevolution in evolutionary economics at least since the neo-Schumpeterian inception four decades ago. In the foundational texts (Dosi et al. 1988; Nelson and Winter 1982), the idea that technological advances, as the key driver of economic change, coevolve with other social forces is already present. Christopher Freeman (1988, p. 2) summarizes some of the key pillars of the (then new) neo-Schumpeterian approach to economic theory by stressing that (1) technological change is the crucial transformative force underlying economic life and socioeconomic change and (2) the institutional framework is inseparable from innovative market dynamics. Moreover, he points to fresh adjustment and adaptation processes that involve an appreciative and empirically persistent notion of coevolution.

Likewise, in Nelson and Winter (1982), as well as in the contribution by Richard Nelson (1988) to the foundational volume by Dosi et al. (1988), Nelson claims that "if technical change is far more complicated and variegated that it is depicted in standard economic theory, so too are the institutional structures supporting it" (Nelson 1988, p. 312). The seed of the coevolutionary approach is also perceptible here. Again, in the same crucial 1988 volume on *Technical Change and Economic Theory*, Dosi and Orsenigo state that technological and institutional change are connected parts of a continuously changing environment (Dosi and Orsenigo 1988, p. 15), an additional appreciation of the same mechanism.

From these pioneering volumes, and developing through a dense and enriching flow of literature that spans from the 1980s to the current 2020s, we find continuous references to the need for interpreting and analyzing the technology–institutional coevolutionary link. As a classical example that culminated in the 1990s, Alfred Chandler's studies on firms' scale and scope highlight how crucial changes in organizational forms and business practices in the nineteenth century coevolved with the railroad and parallel advances in the telegraph technologies. Chandler explains how even specific professional and academic profiles appeared to be shaped by these technologies. Also in the 1990s, James Trevelyan (1992) explored along similar veins the initial stages of robotics. For the same decade, we must also mention the Freeman–Lundvall–Nelson characterization of national innovation systems, a crucial techno-institutional notion that hints at a coevolutionary perspective both in its theoretical developments and in its applications.

Moving on to the twenty-first century, we find the fascinating work by John Peter Murmann (2003). In his classic study about the rise of the modern dyes and the chemical industries in the period from the 1860s to 1918, Murmann provides a clear definition of coevolution. Furthermore, he applies this notion to exploring how German chemical firms, the scientific field of organic chemistry and corporate research labs all linked to the German university system at that time, a coevolution that led to the worldwide industrial leadership of German corporations. More or less at the same time, we also have the well-known episode of the Haber–Bosch process in chemical engineering and the fertilizer industry, in which certain populations of German corporations (including BASF) coevolved with German universities (Leipzig, Karlsruhe) and scientific fields such as electrochemistry, again as sources of leadership. Regarding the innovation systems approaches, a relevant contribution during the decade 2000–2010 was the volume edited by Malerba, Edquist and Steinmueller (2004), a work in which the idea of sectoral systems of innovation was extensively used, applied and connected from an empirical and appreciative viewpoint with the coevolution idea.

More recently, during the decade 2010–2020, we find new applied studies dealing with coevolution in such industries as civil engineering and construction, nanotechnology and medical devices (Bhushan 2017), computers and high-speed contemporary railway transportation systems. For instance, Agrawal (2018) analyzes the emergence of new construction techniques (structural tubular systems to support building forces) as arising from the coevolution of specific firms (e.g. Chicago-based Skidmore, Owings & Merrill), academic institutions in America (e.g. Illinois Institute of Technology) and local authorities. Likewise, in the case of radical innovations in computer software, we find a good example in the development of COBOL (by Grace B. Hopper), which emerged from joint efforts by Hopper, in the US Navy, and private corporations (in close connection with universities). This process was a crucial step in the development of modern software innovations. Finally, we should also mention the study by Pyrgidis (2018) in which we see how the efforts of Liang Jianying – involved in a coevolutionary process between the Chinese authorities, CRRC Quingdao Sifang Co. Ltd. and research teams working around the CR400AF train – have resulted in crucial developments in high-speed train technology.

Following on from the tradition of the aforementioned works, Dosi and Nelson (2010) and Nelson et al. (2018) have synthesized the relevance of the coevolution notion by arguing that this force appears in almost all realms of economic activity: the medical devices sector coevolving with medical practice schools and advanced research hospitals; and electronics and computer hardware and software advances coevolving through and across corporations, intersectoral supply–demand interactions, regulatory agencies and public research programs. Even more recently, we need to explore how digitalized areas of human action coevolve with institutional adaptations, management innovations, consumer options and law (algorithmic trading, advanced aeronautics, GPS applications in smartphones or Google-driven advances toward human virtual reality; see Almudi et al. 2020). Perhaps, the very latest example of coevolution can be seen in the very difficult times of the 2020 Covid-19 pandemic: corporations, government agencies and multinational institutions struggle against time to achieve a safe vaccine, which may be needed to recover our normal socioeconomic lives.

In addition, in parallel to this remarkable interest in the coevolution idea, we also perceive in the literature on evolutionary economics a recurrent and insistent claim for the need to go much deeper in answering questions such as: What does coevolution really (neatly and deeply) mean? How can we operationalize the concept, and can we incorporate it formally in innovation economics and growth models? (Nelson 1995, 2008, 2012, 2018). We detect in the literature a *warning*, according to which neither neoclassical nor evolutionary economics have taken the institutional side of the techno-institutional analysis of change as seriously as they should. Thus, the need to incorporate institutional change in growth theory and industrial dynamic models is recognized as an urgent and crucial task (Witt 2014; Wilson and Kirman 2016; Dosi and Nuvolari 2020).

This is the frame inspiring the content of this third Element in Evolutionary Economics devoted to coevolution in economic systems. We devote the rest of this conceptual section to setting the stage for our work. We begin by presenting some definitions and arguments to support our main statements. The coevolution concept can open up new ways to approach economic change from an evolutionary generalized perspective. To show the operational power of this notion, we devote a significant part of this Element to illustrating how to theorize from a coevolutionary perspective by using neat and tractable formal models. From a methodological angle, we use replicator dynamics models, low-scale ABMs and tractable multilayer settings to develop our work, raising new issues and trying to face significant empirical anomalies (Dosi et al. 2017; Cantner et al. 2019). Thus, we illustrate how the coevolution principle can be of help in unifying complementary mathematical strategies to formalize evolutionary arguments.

Let us note that, even though it is clear that the concepts of evolution and coevolution resemble certain biological counterparts, we use the terms here in a vaguely analogous sense (not in a literal biological sense). Therefore, we are not going to deal in any detail with the biological or epistemological literatures. The reader interested in the psychological, sociological, cultural or biological connections in this work can read the previous Element in this series by Hodgson (2019) or the excellent studies in Foster and Metcalfe (2001), Dopfer (2005),

Dosi et al. (2005), Dopfer and Potts (2008), Witt (2014), Nelson (2018) and the Darwinian approach in Hodgson and Knudsen (2010).

2.1 The Evolutionary Approach to Socioeconomic Change

The idea of representing contemporary capitalist societies as evolving systems has taken shape during the last four decades. It is widely accepted that, under the general heading of *evolutionary economics*, a certain variety of complementary approaches coexist (Nelson and Winter 1982; Dosi et al. 1988; Silverberg and Soete 1994; Metcalfe 1998; Nelson 2008; Winter 2014; Witt 2014; Dollimore and Hodgson 2014; Wilson and Kirman 2016; Dosi and Roventini 2019). Perhaps a common feature of these approaches is that they all characterize capitalist economies as continuously changing from within, through processes that involve the selection of competing organizations and agents, the uneven replication of embodied traits (routines, habits) and the ongoing generation of novelties. In this subsection, we introduce four definitions (capitalist economy, evolving system, replication and selection) to clarify this vision.

2.1.1 Key Preliminary Definitions

We start out by defining the terms capitalist-democratic society, evolving economic system, replication and selection as we discuss these concepts in Almudi and Fatas-Villafranca (2018).

Capitalist-democratic society. We define a contemporary capitalist-democratic society as one in which the right to private ownership is guaranteed; there is an institutional framework guaranteeing freedoms for contracting work, services and exchanges of goods and assets, for business initiatives and for the carrying out of monetary trading; the state has a legitimacy that represents the freely exercised will of citizens and guarantees, among other things, the aforementioned rights and institutional settings; and most productive activities are carried out by private firms, seeking to make monetary profit in the markets.

The evolutionary economics tradition states that the dynamics of these societies can be analytically represented as *evolving complex systems*. These are systems that contain multiple types of heterogeneous agents and entities (firms, consumers, technologies, institutions) interacting with the environment and among themselves, facing a scarcity of resources and struggling to survive and grow. These agents can adapt and/or pass on information to others through imitation and replication processes. Different sources of innovation are observed in these systems and ex post selection processes win out over the novelties that appear. The aggregate outcomes of these systems can be analyzed as emergent properties. Let us briefly define the concepts of an evolving economic system, replication and selection that we will use later on.

Evolving economic system. We define an evolving economic system as a theoretical characterization of economic systems (and, in particular, of modern capitalist societies) according to which heterogeneous agents (firms, consumers, the state) display bounded rationality (Simon 1955, 1957); there is an ongoing endogenous production of novelties; not only markets but also other interaction domains (civil society, populations of competing institutions, the political arena) operate as selection-cum-retention mechanisms; different types of traits embodied in agents with specific intentionality replicate (through learning, imitation, emulation) at uneven rates; and aggregate properties emerge from different arrangements for out-of-equilibrium interactions (Dopfer 2005; Dosi et al. 2005; Hodgson and Knudsen 2010; Markey-Towler 2019).

Replication. This is a specific type of process through which some traits (habits, routines, technologies, norms) of interacting intentional agents diffuse at different rates across the population of agents, under the conditions of causal implication, similarity and information transfer. In the economic use of the term, the different rates of replication of traits across the population depend on how these traits are perceived by agents as providing more or less competitive advantages and/or fitting their specific goals in the specific contexts. As is explained in Almudi and Fatas-Villafranca (2018) the processes of learning, emulation and imitation that usually appear in economic models may be conceptualized as examples of replication in this sense. Applications with a detailed explanation of technicalities for the implementation of this concept can be seen in the models by Fatas-Villafranca et al. (2007, 2009) or within a stochastic evolving network in Fatas-Villafranca et al. (2019).

Selection. Selection in evolving economic systems involves a previous set of entities (firms, civil organizations, institutions) that are transformed into a posterior set, in such a way that all members of the posterior set are sufficiently similar to the members of the anterior set and the resulting shares or population frequencies of posterior entities are positively related with certain domain-specific competitive traits embodied in the agents under selection. These domain-specific traits condition the agents' degree of adaptation to the environment and the fulfillment of their goals and influence the population structures that emerge from competition (these traits include firm technologies, prices, performances, individual skills and habits). Certain implementations of this concept in alternative economic domains can be seen in Fatas-Villafranca et al. (2008, 2009, 2019) and Almudi et al. (2012, 2013, 2017).

Now, if we want to move forward (starting out from these concepts as they have been developed by the evolutionary economics tradition), we propose that we need an extended ontological positioning. One possibility consists of delineating an extended approach that, apart from including as fundamental pillars the aforementioned concepts, may incorporate the notion of *coevolution* as a new coordinating concept. We assume that socioeconomic reality can be conceived as a plurality of (to some extent) self-referential *evolving* domains. However, additionally, we want to stress that we can gain explanatory power if we treat these evolving domains as always dynamically interlinked through mutually shaping innovation, adaptation and selection mechanisms. We believe that it is essential to consider some domains as changing the contexts of others and vice versa, so that the different evolving realms shape each other and are dynamically codetermined (Camprubi 2014; Pretel and Camprubi 2018; Chai and Baum 2019). This ontological positioning can be represented within the realm of evolutionary economic theory by combining (extended) population thinking and by organizing the standard evolutionary concepts through the principle of coevolution.

2.2 Coevolution and the Dynamics of Structurally Distinct Realms

In this brief subsection, we consider the concepts stated in Section 2.1.1 and define a key idea for this Element, that of coevolution. Thus:

> **Coevolution.** We state that two (or more) evolving domains coevolve if these domains causally influence each other in such a way that this multidirectional influence shapes the innovation, replication or selection processes that are specific to each domain. In this way, the multiple evolving realms linked by coevolution are dynamically codetermined.

As we will see, once we adopt this perspective, new possibilities appear. For instance, what used to be considered as the "frozen" parametric environment in previous evolutionary models now becomes endogenous and understandable through the analysis of coevolving systems. Likewise, certain imperfections of selection mechanisms that were often considered as empirical anomalies regarding the predictions of evolutionary economics (replicator dynamics leading to monopoly) are now easily enriched and overcome by the coevolutionary mechanisms involved. Of course, new policy implications appear regarding innovation policy, development policy and market concentration analysis as we move in these directions. Finally, the increase in modeling complexity that some would expect from the coevolutionary approach does not occur. On the contrary, as we find coevolutionary explanations for otherwise stochastic forces in nonlinear systems, the models become more transparent and tractable.

2.3 Methodological Reflections

This Element will illustrate how alternative modeling methodologies can be combined to analyze coevolutionary settings. We believe that an interesting novelty of this work is that we use the concept of coevolution in complementary formal settings. Basically, we use three methodologies:

1. Replicator dynamics models in which coevolving realms are integrated in an overall setting. We explore these types of models by using closed-form analytical resources (sometimes to address the exploration of simplified variants of the global frame) and also by using computational tools. We use this method in a collateral manner in Section 3 and extensively in Sections 4 and 5. To go deeper into the technicalities of these methods, we recommend the mathematical approaches in Hofbauer and Sigmund (1998) and Sandholm (2010) or the detailed applications in Fatas-Villafranca et al. (2011) and Almudi et al. (2012). For those interested in the history-friendly methodology, the models in Fatas-Villafranca et al. (2008, 2009) explore in a replicator dynamics coevolutionary setting the dyes puzzle as explained in Murmann (2003).

2. Low-scale ABMs, in which we not only use computation as a strategy of analysis but also complete this approach with the closed-form analysis of formal parts of the original ABM. We use this approach extensively in Section 3 and in a collateral manner in Section 5. Further explanations of this methodology can be found in Delli Gatti et al. (2018), Nowak (2006) and Fernández-Márquez et al. (2017a). The technicalities from this body of work span from the use of history-friendly models (Malerba et al. 2016) to the exploration of macroeconomic issues (Haldane and Turrell 2019) and certain new developments regarding the evolutionary microfoundations of consumer demand (Fernández-Márquez et al. 2017a, 2017b).

3. Evolving complex networks in which we activate a "downstream" replicator system (Weibull 1995) with an "upstream" low-scale stochastic dynamic network. The idea of dealing with coevolutionary networks is suggested by Vega-Redondo (2007). We use this methodological alternative in Section 3. We try to use a combination of the three alternatives throughout this Element, paying special attention to how suitable they are when dealing with coevolution. We believe that the success of the combination of the aforementioned techniques opens up fresh ways to analyze evolving systems.

3 Coevolution in Markets

We have established in Section 2 that several evolving realms of economic activity coevolve when shaping forces exist that operate across domains affecting the corresponding innovation, replication and selection mechanisms. In this section, we show how this idea can be operationalized to study the coevolution of interlinked industrial sectors. We proceed by proposing a two-sector model in which both sectors coevolve through supply–demand trading interactions, interlinked processes of price formation and bidirectional flows of knowledge. The evolutionary theory of price formation and vertical trading that arises is inextricably engaged with the theory of knowledge creation and innovation diffusion in the model. In this way, our coevolutionary framework combines recent contributions to evolutionary price theory (Bloch and Metcalfe 2018) with the insights into industrial dynamics and innovation policy provided by Schumpeterian economics (Nelson and Winter 1982; Winter 1984; Dosi et al. 1988; Metcalfe 1998; Potts 2000; Metcalfe 2010; Dosi et al. 2017). It also has clear relations with the literature on strategic management (Adner and Kapoor 2010) and with certain studies on the history of technology (Nelson and Sampat 2001; Murmann 2003; Camprubi 2014).

From a theoretical perspective, our two-sector coevolutionary model shows how the innovation capabilities in one sector affect the innovation prospects of another; and we analyze how these relationships flow forwards and backwards across sectors that are continuously in motion. Pricing and trading in the model operate and are affected by multidirectional flows of knowledge. This is fully in line with recent evidence that consistently emphasizes the complexity of market linkages and technological interdependencies (Jacobides et al. 2018). The model also incorporates empirical insights from modern innovation economics (Dosi and Grazzi 2010; Nelson 2012; Nelson 2018). From a policy perspective, the model provides new insights regarding innovation absorptive capacity (Cohen and Levintal 1990; Earl and Potts 2013, 2016; Almudi et al. 2018) and its role in sustainable economic change (Pyka 2017).

Formally, our model builds on Nelson and Winter (1982), Almudi et al. (2013) and Dosi et al. (2013) and consists of a two-sector neo-Schumpeterian setting with an "upstream" machines-producer sector and a "downstream" machines-user sector. Machines are bought by user-firms (operating in Sector 2) from producer-firms (in Sector 1). User-firms buy the machines to produce consumption goods that they sell to final consumers (the demand-side of Sector 2). The modeling strategy we use to implement this scheme is a low-scale ABM. This two-sector approach can be critically compared with previous input–output models (which connect sectors statically through flows of commodities and payments) and with the dynamic general equilibrium models of growth and fluctuations in the neoclassical realm (Aghion and Howitt 1998; Aghion and Griffith 2005). The model also incorporates Schumpeterian mechanisms inherited from the systems of innovation body of works (Freeman 1987; Lundvall 1992; Nelson 1993; Foray et al. 2009).

The model's results may aid in refocusing certain open issues. Thus, an implication of the model is that, while in the simple (but still dominant) basic-science technology-push *plus* property rights frame the practical policy prescription is to target the source of market failures (Bush 1945; Nelson 1959; Arrow 1962a; Trajtenberg 2012), in our coevolutionary framework the market failure targeting may lead to knowledge coordination problems. This will manifest in the misallocation of innovation spending in the cases of low absorptive capacity downstream. Likewise, our model predicts that an unbalanced distribution of policies may produce intersectoral innovation blockages, thus leading to a slowdown in productivity growth or to the collapse of the coevolutionary process. New arguments for current debates have emerged (see Martin and Scott 2000; Gordon 2012; and for sustainability transitions, see Pyka 2017).

In Section 3.1, we present the model – we make continuous reference to Appendix A and to Almudi et al. (2020) for technicalities. We pay special attention to delineating the key processes of replication, innovation, selection and coevolution in the model. We devote Section 3.2 to the analysis of the model, focusing on price theory and knowledge coordination problems. We combine closed-form results of simplified parts of the model with the computational outcomes. In Section 3.3, we extract policy implications and propose further research to develop the approach.

3.1 The Coevolution of Supply and Demand

We propose an agent-based model for a two-sector economy (Dosi et al. 2013; Metcalfe et al. 2006; Saviotti and Pyka 2004, 2013). Each sector consists of a population of heterogeneous firms. In Sector 1, different and gradually improved varieties of a capital good (machines) are produced and sold to Sector 2. In Sector 2, different varieties of a final good are produced by firms and sold to consumers. Firms in downstream Sector 2 buy different varieties of machines from the upstream Sector 1 and produce varieties of the consumption good for final consumers.

Firms producing and offering machines in Sector 1 compete in price and quality (i.e. machine performance). They fix prices according to a modified-pricing rule (Winter 1984) with a mark-up that evolves according to each firm's changing market power and according to each firm's estimates of its close competitors' market power. Each firm then charges an endogenously changing margin on expected unit cost.

Unit cost includes a unit production cost, which is common and constant across firms, and a unit R&D cost (ex ante to fix prices and realized ex post to calculate real ex post profits once the market has operated). R&D intensity in a firm is a firm-specific behavioral trait, as a lagged proportion of profits. Likewise, we model firm performance in Sector 1 as a relative and normalized specific dimension that evolves through innovation. Each firm in Sector 1 produces machines up to the demand point of users from Sector 2.

The demand captured by each firm in Sector 1 probabilistically depends on both the offerings over price and the quality dimensions of its machines. Each firm in Sector 2 buys at most one machine per period of time. Machines fully depreciate and disappear in one period. At any time period, only profitable firms remain. On the other hand, new firms continuously enter the upstream sector, although many will fail.

Sector 2 consists of a changing number of firms due to entry and exit that produce and sell different varieties of a consumption good for final consumers. Sector 2 firms use one machine (bought from Sector 1) to produce their variety of the consumption good, with each quality (variety) of the consumption good dependent on the firm's production technology (the quality of the corresponding machine). Sector 2 firms have a specific knowledge endowment and a degree of absorptive capacity that define its absorption interval. These intervals change with firm experience. Depending on each firm's absorption interval, user-firms observe and assess different parts of the distribution of machines supplied by Sector 1 at any time. They combine price and machine performance from a range of (understandable) options and choose probabilistically. In this way, upstream demand (from downstream firms) dynamically evolves. Once downstream firms buy machines, they set prices and qualities and compete over price and performance to capture final consumers. There is also an ongoing process of firm entry in the downstream sector, although, as with the upstream sector, many entrants will fail. Firms exit if their share in the consumption market falls below 0.005.

Downstream (Sector 2) firms update their knowledge endowments according to the performance level of their most recent machines. Likewise, each downstream firm has, as a specific behavioral trait, what we call a cognitive *radius* when scanning the supply of machines: the higher the radius, the wider the scope of innovative search. Thus, Sector 2 firms have differential absorptive capacity (Cohen and Levintal 1990) as an ability to understand and adopt innovation from Sector 1. Clearly, this absorptive capacity in reality may be constructed over several distinct cumulative mechanisms (Simon 1955, 1991; Nelson and Sampat 2001). Sections 3.1.1 and 3.1.2 formally state the model assumptions, which are synthetically specified in Appendix A.3. We also present in Appendix A3 the values of the base-standard setting for the simulations.

3.1.1 Supply (Sector 1)

Prices and Performance

At time t, we have a changing set of firms in Sector 1: $S_t^1 = \{C_{i,t}^1\}$. We denote by $C_{i,t}^1$ each individual firm i in Sector 1 (superscript 1) at t. These firms produce different varieties of a capital good we call *machine*. We assume boundedly rational profit-seeking firms that compete in price $(p_{i,t})$ and machine performance $(x_{i,t})$ -performance is normalized on the unit interval-. We assume that firms in Sector 1 set prices using an endogenously changing mark-up over expected unit cost. Thus the price set by firm i at t is:

$$p_{i,t} = \mu_{i,t} c_{i,t}^e \tag{1}$$

A novel component of the model is a pricing routine in which the *mark-up* endogenously changes for each firm. We highlight two key aspects. On the one hand, we consider that the higher the expected market share (market power) of each firm, the higher the margin it applies. On the other hand, we state that each firm i delineates at any time the set of her "perceived close rivals" depending on performance distance. The close-rivals' market power at any time moderates the fine-tuning of pricing for each firm. We suppose that the set of "perceived close rivals" is determined according to available information from $t-1$, and is a firm-specific trait. We define this set of "close/direct perceived rivals" as:

$$\Lambda_{i,t} = \{k : |x_{k,t} - x_{i,t}| \le \sigma_i x_t^{max}\}, \sigma_i \in (0,1) \tag{2}$$

In equation (2), we capture each firm's perceived close rivals (or perceived direct competition). Each firm estimates the rivals' overall market power by adding up the market shares of the perceived rivals: $(\sum_{k \in \Lambda_{i,t}} s_{k,t-1})$. If we now consider this intensity of direct competition $(\sum_{k \in \Lambda_{i,t}} s_{k,t-1})$ as an element that can make the demand for the specific machine variety more elastic, it is clear that this factor erodes the perceived market power of the firm. Therefore, considering all the aforementioned points, we assume that the mark-up set by firm i at t, when we consider together (1) each firm's expected market share and (2) the intensity of its perceived direct competition (as a factor that moderates the margin), can be modeled as follows:

$$\mu_{i,t} = \frac{\eta + \sum_{k \in \Lambda_{k,t-1}} s_{k,t-1}}{\eta + \sum_{k \in \Lambda_{k,t-1}} s_{k,t-1} - s_{i,t}^e}, \quad \eta > 1 \tag{3}$$

$s_{i,t}^e = \frac{1}{card(S_t^1)}$ for new firms, and $s_{i,t}^e = s_{i,t-1}$ otherwise.

Finally, regarding the change in firm performance $(x_{i,t})$ we assume that firms improve their machine varieties through technological innovation. We define this in the "Demand-Driven Production and Costs Section," along with how firms determine their R&D spending $(R_{i,t})$.

Demand-Driven Production and Costs

We assume demand-driven production in Sector 1, so that $q_{i,t} = q_{i,t}^d$. Likewise, we assume that total costs include production costs and R&D costs. We consider constant and common unit production costs (c) as firms will differ in their unit R&D efforts. In order to set prices (see equation (1)) firms use ex ante expected unit costs. They must use expected unit costs to fix prices because they still do not know their demand-driven level of production and sales (a level that, as we will see, depends partially on the price). Thus, we assume naïve expectations about the production level, so the expected unit cost is:

$$c_{i,t}^e = c + \frac{R_{i,t}}{q_{i,t}^e} = c + \frac{R_{i,t}}{q_{i,t-1}}, \quad c > 0 \tag{4}$$

Once the structure of demand forms and the exchanges between Sectors 1 and 2 have occurred, firms will know the effective production and the effective unit costs. They will then calculate the real profit for firm i at t, which will be:[1]

$$\pi_{i,t} = (p_{i,t} - c_{i,t})q_{i,t}; \quad c_{i,t} = c + \frac{R_{i,t}}{q_{i,t}} \tag{5}$$

Only profitable firms remain in the market (see Appendix A3).

We also assume that firms devote a *specific proportion of their profits* to R&D with a lag, so that:

$$R_{i,t} = r_i \pi_{i,t-1}, \quad r_i \in (0,1) \tag{6}$$

We often find slightly different R&D spending routines in the literature but all of them render essentially similar results (see Fatas-Villafranca et al. 2008, 2014; Almudi et al. 2012, 2013).

We also suppose that every firm in Sector 2 demands, at most, one unit of a specific variety of the capital good from Sector 1 and uses this unit to produce a consumption good in Sector 2. For simplicity, we assume every unit of capital entirely depreciates and disappears at no cost at the end of each period. When selecting a specific capital-good firm at t, downstream firms assess the

---

[1] The price will be the one given by equation (1) but the effective unit cost to calculate profits will be the one obtained after exchanges.

prevailing levels of price and performance in the upstream Sector 1. In Section 3.2, we specify this process of choice (see also Appendix A3). For now, though, we can see that if we define the set of customers for each firm i at t in Sector 1 as $\Omega_{i,t}$, we have $q_{i,t}^d = card\left(\Omega_{i,t}\right)$.

R&D-Based Innovation

Let $\gamma_{i,t}$ be the flow of new knowledge generated by each firm i in Sector 1 at t. Assume this flow is a random realization of a (truncated) Pareto distribution, so that $\gamma_{i,t} \sim Dist.$, with "*Dist*" representing the truncated Pareto distribution, with supporting values $L = 0$ and $H = 1$. We endogenize the typical Pareto parameter (the slope of the density function θ) so that, $\theta = \frac{1}{\phi \cdot imitation + (1-\phi) \cdot research}$, where (following Nelson 1982; Fatas-Villafranca et al. 2009; Dosi et al. 2017) we have:

$$imitation = \frac{x_t^{max} - x_{i,t}}{x_{i,t}}, \text{ assimilation of external knowledge from}$$

the gap to the frontier;   (7)

$$research = \frac{R_{i,t}}{R_{i,t}^{max}}, \text{ generating knowledge from (normalized) inner R\&D.}$$

In the expressions given by (7) we assume that the productivity of R&D reflected in the flow of new knowledge $\gamma_{i,t}$ depends on both complementary sources, with a sectoral bias denoted by parameter ϕ that determines the relative importance of imitation *versus* innovation efforts within a specific industry. Notice that the lower the firm-specific value of θ at any time, the higher the probability of obtaining a large flow of new knowledge $\gamma_{i,t}$ at that time. Finally, we assume that the relative performance of each Sector 1 firm is updated according to a mechanism in which those firms generating higher-than-average flows of new knowledge, that is, $\gamma_{i,t} - \bar{\gamma}_t > 0$, increase their relative performance compared to rivals in Sector 1. Thus:

$$\frac{x_{i,t+1} - x_{i,t}}{x_{i,t}} = \gamma_{i,t} - \bar{\gamma}_t, \quad \bar{\gamma}_t = \sum_h x_{h,t} \gamma_{h,t}$$ (8)

Firms' Entry/Exit

Firms in Sector 1 with profit $\pi_{i,t} \leq 0$ exit the market. Also, at each time step, one new firm enters the sector. With probability λ, the new firm's traits are selected randomly. Therefore, with probability λ, the new entrant enters into the sector by carrying genuine technological and behavioral novelties. With probability $(1 - \lambda)$, the new firm copies incumbents with probabilities proportional to market shares (Appendix A3).

3.1.2 Demand of Capital Goods and Supply of Consumption Options
(Sector 2)

Overview

At time t, there exists a set of firms in Sector 2, $S_t^2 = \{C_{j,t}^2\}$. Each firm (denoted by j) produces a different variety of consumption goods (with different prices, $p_{j,t}$ and quality levels, $y_{j,t}$). Firms in Sector 2 produce with different techniques or machine‑varieties depending on the technological performances of their respective capital-good providers. The quality of the machines used by firms in Sector 2 determines the corresponding quality of the consumption good supplied to the market. Firms in Sector 2 with superior machines will supply superior-quality consumption goods. Considering the prevailing distribution of machine-performance levels on the supply-side (from Sector 1 at t), and the distribution of cognitive endowments corresponding to the consumption-good firms in Sector 2 $(X_{1,t}, \ldots, X_{card(S_t^2),t})$, each firm j in Sector 2 decides which capital-good firm from Sector 1 it will purchase one machine from; we assume full-capacity use and total depreciation of machines in one period.

Furthermore, for simplicity, the overall production level in Sector 2 is normalized to 1 and fully sold to consumers (the demand-side of Sector 2). The consumption market in Sector 2 is driven by a replicator dynamics equation.

Machine Choice by Each *j*-firm in Sector 2

The process we will now establish is crucial for our model dynamics. We represent the limits of user-firms' absorptive capacity as follows: We assume that each firm is endowed with a firm-specific capacity to understand, incorporate and use new technology. This firm-specific capability depends on each firm's experience but it also rests on the knowledge-base traits of the firm, each firm's culture regarding risk-taking and innovativeness and the different abilities to manage technological absorption and organizational change.

We assume that each firm has, at any time, a specific machine-performance interval capturing what it can understand and assimilate at t. These intervals are distinct among firms and they change and become updated in a path-dependent way as firms learn from using specific machines (Arrow 1962b). As we explain formally in the following paragraphs, we consider that each user-firm j is endowed at t with a specific and changing *absorption interval* defined by a path-dependent *center* $X_{j,t}$ and a specific *understanding radius* $\rho_j \in (0, 1)$.

User-firms care not only about machine performance but also about prices in the process of choice. Thus we consider that firms make their choices from among the set of machines that they can understand and they compare the performances and prices of understandable machines. When they make a purchase, they incorporate the cost of the machine as a cost. This will be the referential on which user-firms charge their margins, to set the prices for final consumption. The quality of the machines determines the quality of the final goods to be sold in Sector 2.

We now formally propose the following process of evaluation and choice for each machine user-firm j in Sector 2:

1. Firm j delimits the set of (cognitively) feasible options, which will be conditioned by the firm-specific cognitive capabilities $\rho_j \in (0, 1)$. This *understanding radius* is a way of parameterizing absorptive capacity in a firm and is therefore a firm-specific trait. Each firm's radius, together with the firm-specific changing center $X_{j,t}$ of the absorption interval, determines the set of feasible providers for firm j, which is $\Xi_{j,t} = \{i : |X_{j,t} - x_{i,t}| \leq \rho_j x_t^{max}\}$
2. Firm j chooses a cognitively feasible type of machine, with a probability that is proportional to $\alpha_1 x_{i,t} + (1 - \alpha_1)\left(1 - \frac{p_{i,t}}{\sum_{k \in \Xi_{j,t}} p_{k,t}}\right), \alpha_1 \in (0, 1)$
3. The quality of firm j becomes $y_{j,t} = x_{i,t}$
4. Each firm in Sector 2 has a cost equal to the price of the machine bought: $c_{j,t} = p_{i,t}$

Since this process takes place for all firms in Sector 2 (Appendix A3), we can define the set of customers for every firm in Sector 1 as:

$$\Omega_{i,t} = \{i - customers\}.$$

Likewise, as long as a firm in Sector 2 uses one specific technological variety of capital good, we assume that this level of performance becomes the firm's cognitive endowment for the next period, that is $X_{j,t+1} = y_{j,t}$.

3.1.3 The Dynamics of the Final Consumption Market

Consider the competition within the downstream sector (Sector 2), with firms competing in price and quality in the consumption-good market. We have already defined how to obtain the quality level of each firm, $y_{j,t}$. Regarding price, we propose that consumption firms also apply a mark-up pricing routine but we now consider a more standard version of the routine that assumes a higher degree of competition in this sector. Then, we just consider:

$$p_{j,t} = \left(\frac{\delta}{\delta - s_{j,t}}\right)c_{j,t}, \quad \delta > 1 \tag{9}$$

In equation (9), $c_{j,t}$ is the cost of the chosen machine and δ (>1) is simply a parameter. As in Winter (1984) or, more recently, in Fatas-Villafranca et al. (2008) and Almudi et al. (2012), we consider that each firm's market share is a good proxy for market power and then it increases its margin. As in Almudi et al. (2013) or Markey-Towler (2016), to represent the market process, we define a competitiveness level for each firm j that combines normalized quality and price:

$$f_{j,t} = \alpha_2 \frac{y_{j,t}}{y_t^{max}} + (1 - \alpha_2)\left(1 - \frac{p_{j,t}}{p_t^{max}}\right); \quad \alpha_2 \in (0,1)$$

It is clear that we are representing both dimensions as related to maximum quality and price in Sector 2 at t. From this fitness indicator, we can now represent the market process in Sector 2 as follows:

$$\frac{s_{j,t+1} - s_{j,t}}{s_{j,t}} = f_{j,t} - \overline{f}_t; \quad \text{with} \quad \overline{f}_t = \sum_h s_{h,t} f_{h,t} \tag{10}$$

For those interested in going deeper into the microfoundations of equation (10) – the demand-side in Sector 2, composed of final consumers – we suggest looking at the evolutionary framework that we suggest in Appendix A1. This discussion can be of help in linking our proposal to the industrial dynamics literature and also in connecting our model with the evolutionary game theory approach.

Firms' Entry/Exit

Firms in Sector 2 with a share lower than 0.005 leave the market, while at each time step one new firm enters the sector. The new entrant may bring novel traits or it may copy one of the incumbents (see Appendix A3). Regarding these two possibilities, we consider that with probability λ (a *mutation rate*) the new entrant *carries fully novel traits*. On the other side, with probability $1 - \lambda$ the new entrant *copies* one of the incumbent firms.

In the case of *fully new entrants* (with probability λ), an original element of the model is that we assume that these fully new entrants in the downstream sector randomly draw, as a specific feature, their *understanding-cognitive radius* from a *Beta distribution* with positive parameters (a, b). Note that the Beta distribution is a family of continuous probability distributions defined by two positive shape parameters (a, b). These parameters appear as exponents in the random variable and thereby control the shape of the distribution.

More precisely, as shown by Stachurski (2016), the probability density function (pdf) for the Beta distribution is:

$$f(\rho) = \begin{cases} \left[\dfrac{1}{B(a,b)}\right]\rho^{a-1}(1-\rho)^{b-1}, & (0 < \rho < 1), \quad a, b > 0. \\ 0, \, otherwise \end{cases}$$

$$\text{With } B(a,b) = \int_0^1 \rho^{a-1}(1-\rho)^{b-1}d\rho \tag{11}$$

Note with ρ we mean the cognitive radius, and parameters (a,b) determine the shape of the Beta distribution (equation (11)) in alternative settings. We consider this distribution because it allows us to represent a wide range of scenarios regarding the institutional structure engendering machine-user firms with different degrees of *absorptive capacity* (in Almudi et al. 2020, we show the versatility of the Beta distribution depending on alternative parametric combinations of (a,b) to represent formally Uniform, Power Law, Truncated Normal or Negative exponential generative stochastic processes).

This approach allows us to represent the effects of more or less skewed generative structures, which will be our proxy to characterize alternative institutional systems from which more or less absorptive *fully new* user-firms emerge. We note that the expected value and variance of a Beta distribution, given $a > 0$, $b > 0$, are $E = \frac{a}{a+b}$ and variance $Var = \frac{ab}{(a+b)^2(a+b+1)}$

We also bring out the notion of the *skew* of the *Beta pdf* that we will use in alternative simulations (with positive skew meaning a right-tailed distribution, negative skew meaning a left-tailed distribution or zero skew indicating perfect symmetry). This *skew* of the Beta distribution (equation (11)) (which we denote by ζ) is a function of the parameters (a,b); it is the normalized third-order moment of the Beta pdf, which can also be approached through the well-known mean–median relationship to measure skewness. We can play with alternative values of (a,b), leading to alternative values for the corresponding skew ζ. Later in this section, we discuss the way in which the Beta skew ζ (being negative, null or positive in alternative parametric settings, as defined by alternative values of (a,b)) has an effect on our model outcomes. Owing to the limited scope of this Element, we draw on the technical analysis carried out in Almudi et al. (2020). Here, we simply illustrate the synthesizing fruitfulness of the coevolution notion, and we obtain a few new results. In Almudi et al. (2020), we have detected significant statistical fits relating certain emergent properties of our model (firm's average R&D efforts in limit states or the probability of collapse of the whole coevolutionary industrial dynamics) and the values of (a,b) and ζ that shape the institutional frame in alternative simulation settings. In this Element, we go deeper into the interpretation of those results and obtain additional insights into price theory.

Finally, to close the presentation of the model, we assume that, in those cases in which (with probability $(1 - \lambda)$) the *entrant firm copies one of the incumbents*, this imitative process takes place randomly with probabilities proportional to prevailing market shares. We assume that the initial market share of the new entrant is 0.005, with other market shares being recalculated accordingly.

3.2 Prices, Knowledge Creation and Change in Coevolutionary Environments

Our model is suitable for addressing many different research questions. In fact, we propose it as a general framework to carry out complementary research lines dealing with the determinants of prices and industrial dynamics, industrial ecologies and sectoral ecosystems, price routines as a part of firm theory and economic growth with innovation policy. Nevertheless, considering the limited scope of this Element, we only show how to use the model as a tool for future research works around *specific questions*. For instance: To what extent can intersectoral knowledge coordination problems be responsible for systemic failures in this coevolutionary framework? What is the specific role of firm absorptive capacity (represented by firm absorption intervals and the generative Beta pdf) in these processes? Do these processes have something to do with emergent prices?

To tackle these questions within our model, let us begin by explaining that the model is implemented in JAVA and the statistical analysis is carried out with R-Project. The model dynamics reach limit (stationary) states in approximately 5,000 periods, which is the time span to stationary situations that we have obtained through several methods, including the Kolmogorov–Smirnov (K–S) test (see Fernández-Márquez et al. 2017a, 2017b). Because of stochasticity, we run the model 100 times and average the data for each setting of parametric values. In Almudi et al. (2020), we fully explain the technicalities of the simulations.

3.2.1 The Beta (a,b) Component of the Institutional Frame and the Viability of Multisectoral Coevolution in Innovative Environments

In our model, the absorptive capacity of the downstream sector depends on the alternative generative structures *Beta* (a,b) (with varying shapes and skew ζ depending on parameters (a,b)). As we explained in 3.1, we can pose alternative shapes of the Beta (a,b) distribution (in different simulation settings) to represent alternative institutional frameworks from which new (downstream) user-firms are drawn. We can relate these frames to the role of national universities, different training and regulatory frameworks, R&D programs and professional associations leading to more or less absorptive firms.

As a first approach to our results, we analyze the influence of the *skewness* of the Beta (a,b) distribution on the emergent *probability of technological overshooting* (Earl and Potts 2013, 2016), or what we call the *probability of collapse* in the model. As a measure of potentially unsustainable coevolutionary paths emerging in the model, we calculate the probability of collapse owing to technological overshooting for each setting as the average number of times in which either Sector 1 or Sector 2 vanishes during the 100 initial steps of the average run. The probability of collapse that we obtain for each parametric setting enables us to obtain a base of simulation data from which the mechanism connecting absorptive capacity in the downstream sector to innovation overshooting in the upstream sector can be analyzed (Almudi et al. 2020).

Thus, our first computational analysis consists of relating the probability of collapse in the model to specific shapes of the density function for the Beta (a,b) in Sector 2. We run the model for different initial conditions and parametric values. Specifically, we depart from what we call in Appendix A3 the *base-setting* and we run the model for $79 \times 79 = 6{,}241$ different parametric combinations.

From the database that we obtain from this computational procedure, we can analyze the explicative power of the parameters (a, b) and also the explanatory significance of the skewness ζ of the Beta distribution as regressors for the probability of collapse by technological overshooting.

We use the data obtained from the simulations of the model to estimate a statistical relation linking the probability of collapse in the model (P) and the shape of the Beta distribution from which we depart in each case – which is determined by parameters (a,b). The best fit that we obtain for this relation in Almudi et al. (2020) is for a function such as:

$$P(a,b) = \beta_0 + \beta_1 a + \beta_2 a^2 + \beta_3 a^3 + \beta_4 b + \beta_5 ab + \beta_6 a^2 b + \beta_7 b^2 + \beta_8 ab^2 + \beta_9 b^3.$$

The specific values that we estimate from our simulation data for this expression are:

$$P(a,b) = 0.021 - 0.02a + 0.00614a^2 - 0.000465a^3 + 0.0098b - 0.00319ab$$
$$+ 0.000239a^2 b - 0.00019b^2 + 0.000052ab^2 - 0.00000227b^3$$

As we explain in Almudi et al. (2020), the confidence intervals for the fit-estimates, and the very low values we obtain for the p-values, indicate the high statistical significance of the regressors. Likewise, regarding the quality of the statistical estimation, the confidence intervals are narrow and the indicator $R_{adjusted} = 0.9168$ is very high for the cubic polynomial. Thus, we have a very good fit and a significant statistical relation linking probability of collapse – through a cubic polynomial – with (a,b) parameters of the Beta distribution in the model.

This fit is just a first indicator regarding the key role that the Beta distribution may play in allowing or not for a smooth multisector coevolutionary process. To sharpen our results, we check whether the skewness (*skew* ζ) of the Beta distribution is a good candidate to explain (in a more compact and understandable manner), the probability of collapse. The best fit for this emergent property within our model is a polynomial regression with the skew of the Beta distribution as a key explanatory variable determining the probability of collapse. As we discuss in detail in Almudi et al. (2020), the specific functional form capturing the relation between probability of collapse for the overall coevolutionary process and the Beta skew that we find is:

$$P(\zeta) = \varphi_0 + \varphi_1\zeta + \varphi_2\zeta^2 \tag{12}$$

Further, the specific estimated values that we obtain lead to the following result:

$$P(\zeta) = 0.0066425 + 0.01192869(\zeta) + 0.00402343(\zeta)^2$$

Equation (12) and its statistical fit represent an emergent global property of the model dynamics. It is not the result of a single run; it is a synthesis obtained from the data generated from thousands of runs of the model, runs that arise from the systematic computation of the model departing from the plausible values in Appendix A3. Note that equation (12) and its numerical fit from our simulation results show that a higher skew ζ (a more right-tailed Beta distribution) increases in a quadratic manner the probability of collapse because of knowledge coordination problems. Considering equation (12), we can infer that, as we move from skew values "0" upwards to positive values, we see that positive skew ($\zeta > 0$) (right-tailed) shapes of the Beta distribution clearly increase the probability of collapse. The innovative capacity of Sector 1 (upstream) overshoots the absorptive capacity of the downstream sector (Sector 2). On the other side, for negative skew ($\zeta < 0$) (left-tailed) distributions, the probability of collapse is basically null. In economic terms, we can say that right-tailed Beta distributions represent institutional generative-frames that are somehow ineffective in engendering permeable machine-user firms in Sector 2. Thus, the outcomes of the model simulations reveal that we get a *fastly increasing* probability of collapse when we fix institutional settings with low capacity for creating dynamically capable machine users in Sector 2 (right-tailed Beta distributions).

Formally, equation (12) indicates that, when we run the model from settings in which we consider strictly convex (right-tailed and very close to the vertical axis) Beta distributions as generative structures of user-firms in Sector 2, the probability mass is mostly concentrated on low radius. Therefore, the low adaptability and low cognitive-understanding capacity of user-firms imply a higher probability of collapse. Conversely, with peak-shaped left-tailed Beta distributions, the probability mass is concentrated on higher values for the radius (high absorptive capacity) and we then get lower probabilities of collapse. The computational results show that right-tailed distributions lead to a high probability of collapse. Conversely, left-tailed Beta pdfs eliminate collapse.

According to what we have found, our model implies that innovation policy should target increasing knowledge not only where original producer-innovation takes place (Sector 1) but also at the level of the user-sector. This is a new perspective that is different from taxing, subsidies, neoclassical market failure corrections or picking winners. The need to promote absorptive capacity at the downstream level to reduce blocking factors at the upstream level is clear in our coevolution model.

As a more intuitive insight into the importance of (a,b) and the skew of the Beta distribution in our model, and in order to link the discussion in this section with the discussion in the following paragraphs, we present in Figures 1 and 2 two illustrative representative graphs that seek to make a bit clearer the preceding results. We have picked up representative runs of the model (departing from the base-setting in Appendix A3), and we show the *average level of R&D spending* and innovative effort that emerge in Sector 1 as well as the underlying emergent value of the *average understanding radius* in Sector 2 for alternative values of parameters (a,b) leading to opposite signs of the Beta skew. In Figures 1 and 2, we fix all the parameter values as in Appendix A3, except for (a,b). In Figures 1 and 2, we fix the values $a = 1$ and $b = 3$, which, according to equation (11), determine a right-tailed (positive skew) Beta distribution. We assume in Figures 1 and 2 that the supporting institutional structure generating user-firms in Sector 2 is not good; it tends to generate user-firms in Sector 2 with low absorptive capacity.

In Figures 1 and 2, there appear two significant results. First, we have depicted the series up to step $t = 97$ because, at that instant, the model generates

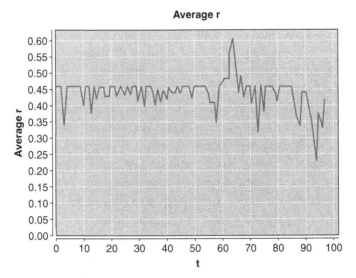

Figure 1 Average R&D-to-profit ratio in Sector 1 (time evolution) ($a = 1$, $b = 3$)

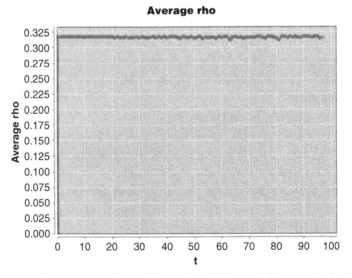

Figure 2 Average understanding radius in Sector 2 (time evolution)
($a = 1$, $b = 3$)

a collapse. Second, in Figure 2, we show that the average understanding radius quickly stabilizes at 0.322. Both results are related. The low level that emerges for the average radius is the causal factor of the sudden collapse at $t = 97$. Thus, there is a time in which technological overshooting happens and the process stops.

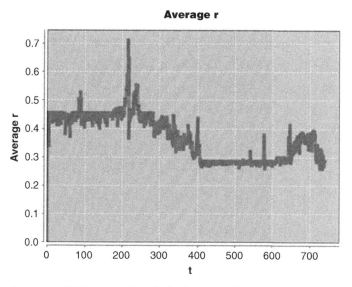

Figure 3 Average R&D-to-profit ratio in Sector 1 (time evolution) ($a = 5, b = 1$)

To see this, we can now present the representative runs that we obtain from the model for a left-tailed (negative skew) Beta distribution (we fix $a = 5$, $b = 1$) with the rest of the parametric values being those in Appendix A3. Notice that, from equation (11), the institutional structure supporting user-firms in Sector 2 that we are fixing is now much more effective than the one underlying Figures 1 and 2. We now obtain Figures 3 and 4.

Drawing on Figures 3 and 4, we would like to mention three important results. First, by looking at Figure 4 we observe that the average understanding radius that emerges in Sector 2 is now 0.79, much higher than the value in Figure 2. That is, the underlying Beta generative structure (left-tailed pdf) ends up generating much more absorptive machine-user firms. Second, we no longer obtain the two-sector collapse. The process develops until it stabilizes. A much more effective Beta-supporting structure is crucial for coevolution to develop. Finally, in this new setting in which the Beta generative structure allows for the process to proceed, we observe in Figure 3 a much more vibrant industry coevolution. There are phases in which high R&D-to-profit ratios endogenously emerge. Sector 1 matures little by little since the absorptive capacity of users downstream allows for the coevolutionary process to cover different industry life stages. This result can also be seen in the evolution of the *number of firms in both sectors* for this setting (with a left-tailed Beta distribution and nice supporting institutions generating absorptive capacity in Sector 2), as we show in Figure 5. The joint coevolution of the number of firms in both sectors

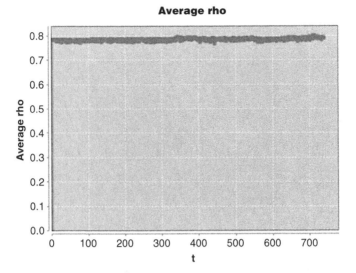

Figure 4 Average understanding radius in Sector 2 (time evolution)
$(a = 5, b = 1)$

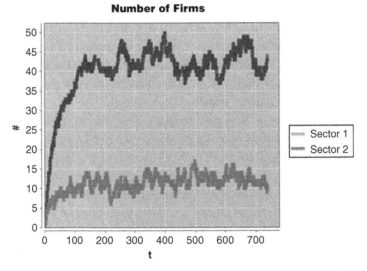

Figure 5 Number of firms in both sectors (time evolution) $(a = 5, b = 1)$

flows as time passes. Sector 1 generates a more concentrated (oligopolistic) structure. Meanwhile, Sector 2 generates a more atomistic structure, a higher number of firms and more volatility (more turmoil in the entry/exit of firms). Let us connect these results with a more refined analysis in the following section. We will also deal (at least briefly) with the formation of prices in our two-sector coevolution model.

3.2.2 Innovation, Prices and Economic Change

We wonder now whether the overall innovativeness of our system (as measured by the *intensities in firm-R&D* in the model) may be related to the shape of the *Beta* (a,b) institutional generative pattern in Sector 2 *as a global property*. As we will see, we obtain that the skew of the Beta distribution appears again as a crucial factor that globally guides the overall pattern of R&D in the model. We will also explore the formation of prices.

Notice that, in our coevolutionary model, firm-specific R&D-to-profit ratios are the key behavioral engines that explain innovation efforts and technological change in the upstream sector. Note also that the distribution of these firm-specific ratios r_i at any time, and the average R&D ratio $\overline{r}_t = \sum_i s_{i,t} r_i$ in Sector 1 at t, are dynamic emergent properties dependent on the overall functioning of the model. We have briefly illustrated this fact in Figures 1–4. Now, we want to study whether we might detect *global regularities* in the computational results of the model, connecting R&D intensity (given by $\overline{r}_t$) in the upstream innovative sector and the Beta generative distribution in the downstream sector; and we explore this property by considering the *skewness of the Beta (a,b) distribution in Sector 2, as a good potential target to explain the emergent limit-stationary value of* $\overline{r}_t = \sum_i s_{i,t} r_i$

The analysis in Almudi et al. (2020) already revealed a surprising result that we called the *slump effect* in the model. The statistical analysis of the computational outcomes of our model reveals that we get a very significant reversed-sigmoidal fit for the limit-stationary data of the average R&D spending effort in Sector 1, $\overline{r}_t = \sum_i s_{i,t} r_i$ emerging from alternative settings in terms of the skew ζ of the Beta (a,b) distribution in Sector 2. The model reaches stationarity in 5,000 steps. As we justify in detail in Almudi et al. (2020), the specific functional formal that is significant when dealing with this relationship is:

$$\overline{r} = \frac{\psi_0}{1 + e^{\psi_1 \cdot \zeta - \psi_2}} + \psi_3 \tag{13}$$

We obtain a fit in which all the parameters in equation (13) are positive. More precisely, the specific statistical fit that we get is (Almudi et al. 2020):

$$\overline{r} = \frac{0.0546695}{1 + e^{3.0831232 \cdot \zeta - 0.1610722}} + 0.0584723$$

Then, note in equation (13) with its fit departing from negative skew (highly left-tailed and effective) distributions in Sector 2 (in horizontal axis), we obtain in correspondence high average R&D-to-profit ratios in

Sector 1 in the stationary limit of the dynamics. High levels of $\bar{r}_t = \sum_i s_{i,t} r_i$ in the innovative (upstream) Sector 1 spontaneously emerge. Thus, we need left-tailed shapes in Beta (a,b) in Sector 2 for high R&D-to-profit ratios in upstream sectors to emerge. Institutional structures that are dense in probability with relatively high absorptive capacity in the downstream sector drive profitability in the upstream sector. As a policy model, this means that, to increase the return to R&D in Sector 1, we need to boost absorptive capacity in Sector 2.

Likewise, a decreasing relationship leading to lower values for $\bar{r}_t = \sum_i s_{i,t} r_i$ in Sector 1 in terms of increasing Beta (a,b) skew is clear in equation (13) and the corresponding statistical fit. The higher the right-tailedness (positive skew) of the Beta generative structure in Sector 2 (ineffective supporting institutions downstream), the lower the R&D intensity and propensity to innovate in Sector 1. Let us note that, because of the inverse S-shaped pattern in equation (13) and its fit, the range of change (or the sensitivity) in the emergent values for $\bar{r}_t$ to changes in skew ζ is very large. This is so since equation (13) is a highly nonlinear functional form which represents, within our model, the underlying existence of "slump effects" linking emergent levels of innovativeness to the profile of the supporting institutional structure from which downstream users are generated.

What is very relevant in this result is what we have called the *slump effect* of R&D intensity as related to *skew ζ* in equation (13). More precisely, the inverted sigmoidal shape in equation (13) indicates that, as the generative structure in the downstream sector becomes less able to create downstream absorptive capacity (as Beta (a,b) becomes more right-tailed), there are slight initial reductions in $\bar{r}_t$. Eventually, however, we may reach a point of skew from which $\bar{r}_t = \sum_i s_{i,t} r_i$ decreases sharply. This is the slump effect. In our model, absorptive capacity in the user-sector influences in a highly nonlinear manner the R&D-to-profit emergent ratio in the innovative upstream sector; and the process develops in a coevolutionary manner. We dig much deeper into this effect in Almudi et al. (2020).

The model suggests that the user-firm's capability to understand and assimilate innovations is crucial in generating *spontaneous* and *voluntary* increases in the levels of R&D and innovation carried out by machine-producers in the upstream sector. This is a very important result that poses additional arguments in favor of procurement policies capable of unchaining technological progress with no need to rely on taxes, picking winners, subsidies and other traditional policies. Furthermore, our model detects the dangerous possibility that the mechanisms underlying innovation slowdowns may be highly nonlinear (the *slump effect*). In these cases, even moderate deteriorations of the institutional frames may have only minor effects in the innovation rates; but, unexpectedly, equation (13) a slightly higher deterioration of the generative structure near the inflection zone can produce a very intense decrease in innovativeness.

We now would like to pay attention very briefly to the *price dynamics* that may emerge from our coevolution model. Of course, price theory in innovative frames, from an evolutionary perspective, is a whole line of research in itself (see Bloch and Metcalfe 2018). Therefore, we will simply suggest how this problem can be tackled from our coevolution model in two complementary steps: First, we will obtain a closed-form result (from a simplified variant of the model) that will spotlight our computational search. Second, we will illustrate with a computational result how the simple result regarding sectoral prices formation can be generalized.

Let us begin by stating a proposition referring to the price dynamics within Sector 2 (the downstream-user sector that produces consumption goods but that is also the demand-side of the market upstream, in Sector 1). For simplicity, let us assume that Sector 2, in the specific case of equation (10), is fully biased to price competition. For the sake of a preliminary exploration, we freeze some aspects of the dynamics in such a way that the number of consumer firms remains constant (n in Sector 2) and have constant and common unit costs equal to 1. Likewise, we analyze the dynamics for pricing routines in the continuous time version of the model in the form

$$p_i(t) = 1 + \alpha_i s_i(t), \quad i = 1, \ldots, n$$

Notice that this routine can be reached through a linear Taylor expansion of equation (9) in the general model. The results that follow are qualitatively similar for positive real values between 0 and 1 (as is the case for market shares). The continuous time version for the price competition version of equation (10), with the linearized pricing routines driving competition in Sector 2 can be restated as:

$$\dot{s}_i = \beta s_i(t)\left[\sum_{j=1}^{n} s_j(t)p_j(t) - p_i(t)\right]$$

$$p_i(t) = 1 + \alpha_i s_i(t), \quad i = 1, \ldots, n$$

(14)

Then, looking at the system given by equation (14) as a simplified variant of the complex dynamics of Sector 2 in the general model, we will obtain a result, shown in Proposition 3.1, that is highly significant for the general version of the model. We look for possible interior resting points in the market process driven by the system defined in equation (14). Note that the dynamics of the system presented in equation (14) develop on the unit-simplex Δ^n and both the boundary and interior of Δ^n are invariant sets (Sandholm 2010). Thus, in Proposition 3.1, we focus on the interior of the simplex, although it is clear that there will still be resting points at the faces, edges and vertices of the simplex. For the sake of economic significance and given what we have observed in the simulations presented in Section 3.2.1, we focus on the interior of the simplex. Since the interior is invariant, and we will always run the analysis from the interior of the simplex (let us denote it by Δ^n), then we are interested in the possible existence and stability of interior resting points. If this were the case, we would focus the computational analysis with this finding in mind. Proposition 3.1 synthesizes the key result for the case of n firms in Sector 2. We present the proof of this proposition in Appendix A2.

Proposition 3.1

The general (dimension n) replicator system (14) has a unique equilibrium point $s^* \in D = Int(\Delta^n)$. This point s^* is globally asymptotically stable within D.

Proof See Appendix A2.

This proposition allows us to explain why, in the simulations of the general version of the coevolution model, we very often find convergence toward a market situation in which several (often many) firms share the market (both in Sector 2 and, upstream, in Sector 1). Furthermore, Proposition 3.1 shows that this emergent *imperfect selection* in our two-sector coevolutionary process is not due to the ongoing entry/exit mechanism in the model. It is due to the fact that, if we model market selection through replicator systems with endogenous fitness levels, and we consider what evolutionary economics explains regarding organizational routines (hereby pricing routines), then replicators – in general – *do not select just one contender*. This result is relevant for recent controversies regarding whether the empirical results (with seemingly imperfect selection not eliminating all the rivals but one) are compatible with the replicator dynamics or not (Dosi and Nelson 2010). We state that there is no contradiction between empirics and the theory. There is no empirical reason to reject the replicator selection mechanism in our evolutionary theoretical analysis just because we observe seemingly imperfect selection outcomes in real industries.

Moving on from the methodological insight in Proposition 3.1, and drawing on the guiding result in the proposition that indicates that prices in the model may, in general, emerge from interior limit states within the market-simplex, we present now an illustrative computational outcome for the general version of the model. Regarding price formation, our model generates situations that are

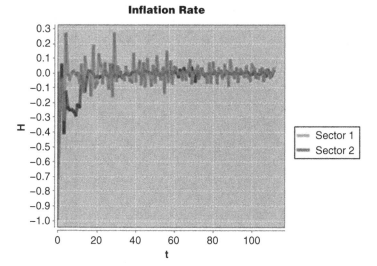

Figure 6 Dynamics for the rate of change of the average price in both sectors

perfectly compatible with the result in Proposition 3.1 for the simple variant of the model. Owing to the limited scope of this Element, we simply present an illustrative (but representative) computational outcome. We want to focus on how the dynamics of prices in both sectors converge because of two-sector coevolution. With this in mind, let us denote by H_1 and H_2 the inflation rate in each sector, defined as the rate of change of the average price in each sector from one period to the next. We can then represent the time series that emerges from simulating the model (for the rate of average price change in both sectors) in one representative run. We do not now bias the skew of the Beta distribution. We consider $a = b = 1$ (that is, perfect symmetry, skew 0, as in Appendix A3) and we maintain the other values in Appendix A3.

Figure 6 shows how the rate of change of the average price in both sectors converges and tends toward a limit-value; this value corresponds to a situation akin to what we showed in Proposition 3.1 as being an interior stationary state of the market within the simplex. In Figure 7, we present the way in which the number of firms in both sectors coevolve.

In Figure 7, we see how the convergent dynamics for the rate of price change in Figure 6 emerge from two-sector coevolution, leading to an interior point in terms of market shares, a situation in which the markets end up being populated by several (even many) firms. Of course, the analysis could proceed much further, but we prefer to highlight this line of inquiry as a potential path for future research.

Figure 7 Dynamics for the number of firms in both sectors

3.3 Multisectoral Coevolution and Imperfect Selection

We have made operational the general notion of coevolution by proposing a two-sector ABM model. It is clear that this model can be considered as a stylized representation to understand such processes as those explored in Foray et al. (2009), Bushan (2017), Agrawal (2018) and Cantner et al. (2019). The key point of our model is that the cognitive alignment of knowledge creation and absorption capabilities among the innovation trajectories of Sector 1 and Sector 2 is complex because absorptive capacity constraints in the downstream sector can back-propagate to cause overshooting from the upstream sector. Although we have decided to make *coevolution in markets* operational by modeling a two-sector process, we find very interesting coevolution aspects in other contributions in the literature: the vertically integrated dynamic value chains in Cantner, Savin and Vannuccini (2019); or the analysis of sustainable paths toward a green economy in Pyka (2017) and Urmetzer et al. (2018).

In addition, we think that some of our coevolutionary results are of direct relevance for posing the innovation problem as a meso-problem of multisectoral knowledge coordination, in line with Dopfer and Potts (2008). In this sense, our model suggests a new policy framework that may help us make sense of the widely observed low productivity performance of modern innovation policy as a consequence of sectorally unbalanced knowledge and the presence of frictions in intersectoral coevolution. In our model, the *innovation policy problem* lies in aligning innovation and absorptive capacity in a two-sector nonlinear stochastic complex framework. In this regard, the slump effect, according to which improving the generative structures in downstream sectors could have sharp positive effects in stimulating R&D and innovation in the upstream sectors, highlights a possibility for improving the performance of innovation policy in the near future.

Finally, we would like to suggest that, in order to reinforce the resilience of certain sectors in some nations, which have failed badly during the contemporary Covid-19 pandemic, the coevolution model presented may be of help. In certain nations in which a process of reindustrialization and overall reconstruction are needed after the destruction caused by the pandemic, the key role of technologically sophisticated user-sectors (Sector 2 in our model) and the building up of supporting institutional structures (the Beta distribution) must be considered. Top-down innovation policies are not enough. The process of reconstruction must be taken as it is: a complex uncertain process that must put in motion a system conformed by intra-subsystems that should end up *coevolving* smoothly. We believe that the previously presented framework can be of great help in this endeavor.

4 Coevolution of Technology and Institutions: Growth

As we have explained in Sections 2 and 3, evolutionary economics claims that the technology-driven self-transformation of market economies is a fundamental aspect of social change (Nelson and Winter 1982; Dosi and Nelson, 2010). It is well known that different realms of activity differ in their patterns of change; but it remains clear that attempts to improve the way we do things, as well as efforts to solve new problems, go on everywhere in modern economies (Metcalfe 1998). This is a key driver of economic growth (Saviotti and Pyka 2004; Ciarli et al. 2019).

In this section, we explore the statement that human understanding in specific realms and science-related institutions and the efforts to improve technical practice in organized fields of activity coevolve (Nelson 2018). In this regard, we analyze why smooth coevolution processes fostering technological advance are not always the case.

In order to develop these arguments and the corresponding policy implications, we organize this section as follows: In Sections 4.1 and 4.2, we explore some of the processes underlying technological change that involve the coevolution between agents devoted to technical practice, institutions and specific bodies of understanding. We propose a stylized growth model in which we use the principle of *coevolution* as a synthetic device to deal with the aforementioned sources of change (Fatas-Villafranca et al. 2008; 2009; Almudi et al.

2012, 2017). The model suggests important reflections on the complex role of policy-makers within coevolutionary environments (Murmann, 2003; Nelson 2008; Witt, 2009). In Section 4.3, we then draw on the results obtained in Sections 4.1 and 4.2, and, by incorporating new concepts such as fuzzy sets (Zadeh 1965) and choice structures (Gilboa 2004), we propose an approach to decision-making (in coevolutionary settings) that may support innovative action in science and technology policy (Foray et al. 2009; Trajtenberg 2012). The results are not only useful for policy-makers; they can also be used by innovative firms and other agents when coevolutionary processes of a certain kind seem to be at work. We then combine the results in Sections 4.1, 4.2 and 4.3 to obtain a statistical index (the $\mathcal{T}$-Index) capable of assessing the operation of coevolutionary engines in specific realms. We illustrate how policy-makers can use the index for science and technology policy; allocating resources among alternative R&D paths; or when facing choice within radically uncertain environments. We also link our analysis to discussions on the economics of development as a learning process.

4.1 Coevolution of Practice, Institutions and Understanding

Recent evolutionary contributions to the economics of innovation point out that the classical Arrow–Nelson approaches to technology policy (Nelson 1959, 1962; Arrow 1962a) ignore important elements that are inherent to the processes of technological advance (Metcalfe 2010; Dosi and Grazzi 2010; Dosi and Nelson 2010; Almudi, Fatas-Villafranca, Jarne and Sanchez 2020). Radical uncertainty in innovative environments seems to preclude the use of strict versions of the optimization hypothesis. Likewise, heterogeneity of agents, bounded rationality, domain-specific selection and learning, all lead to ruling out the analytical prevalence of the sectoral market equilibrium methodology as a fundamental pillar of innovation studies. Finally, mutually dependent selection processes at work at different levels shed doubts on the suitability of dynamic general equilibrium models and aggregate formalisms as workhorses for the economics of innovation and growth. At least for these reasons, neo-Schumpeterian evolutionary economics has been proposing new theoretical arguments and methods that may be more compatible with the challenges to technology policy and growth posed by contemporary self-transforming environments.

In this section, we develop a *coevolutionary analysis* along the lines of previous models we have presented in Fatas-Villafranca et al. (2008) and Almudi et al. (2012, 2017). Advanced technical tools to dig into the models are used in Fatas-Villafranca et al. (2011). In this section, and considering the scope of this Element, we do not want to deal with the technicalities. Rather, we prefer to explain as neatly as possible what we mean by coevolution of institutions and technology in the study of economic growth and then look for clear policy implications regarding the sources of growth.

4.1.1 Technology

When we talk about *a specific technology*, we hereby refer to a range of technical and scientific integrated bodies of knowledge (natural principles, concepts, cause–effect relations) embodied in processes, products and organizational forms, which allow humans to solve a specific problem P in a certain way, at time t, and which generate a frontier of efficiency and/or performance in practice. As examples, we can think about different bridge-building technologies, irrigation techniques or alternative means of storing energy. *A specific technology* and its corresponding frontier level can advance; the technology can be widely used across diverse and changing places (firms, hospitals, organizations, households, regions); the technology often operates at below-the-frontier levels of practice; technologies change and eventually decline and disappear (Fatas-Villafranca et al. 2012). In general, technological progress can be represented as a coevolutionary process of knowledge renewal, emerging from practice, research, new applications and institutional and organizational reconfigurations, all interacting at different stages of proximity from the final action.

4.1.2 Coevolution of Practice, Institutions and Understanding

When we talk about the coevolution of practice and understanding driving technological advance, we refer to mutually connected selection processes at work that involve:

1. The realm of current *practices within a field*, that is to say, how something is being done across diverse spots of practice (firms, public organizations) and lines of advance but also how current practice within a certain paradigm in the field *evolves*.
2. The realm of emergent *understandings*, that is, how the way we do things and fix problems is becoming conceptualized, better represented and often understood (in basic and applied sciences developed at specific institutions) and used accordingly. A certain body of understanding develops unevenly across heterogeneous locations of research: institutes, universities, corporate labs.

We take from neo-Schumpeterian evolutionary economics the idea that both the bodies of practice and the bodies of understanding (materialized in distinct organizations and institutions) evolve (in the sense that they endogenously develop according to the principles of internal variation, retention/replication and competitive selection). Furthermore, we want to emphasize here that, in fact, these bodies of implemented practices and understandings *coevolve*, in the sense that selection, replication and innovation processes operating in these realms are mutually dependent and become mutually codetermined.

Regarding all the aforementioned, there is a specific finding that we want to integrate in our analysis below – namely, if we consider Sarewitz and Nelson (2008a, 2008b) and Almudi et al. (2016), we can establish *three rules* that may allow us to detect blocking and/or catalyst factors operating within the specific coevolutionary processes driving technological advance in different realms of activity. We suggest that these rules may be of great help in monitoring and even assessing alternative technological trajectories in such crucial domains as medical practices; modern aircrafts or robotics; computer hardware, software and the implementation of digital technologies; financial services; and the development of technologies within more sustainable innovation systems.

These three *principles or rules* are the following:

1. The *cause–effect* rule (R1): If the link between what a technology does and providing a solution to a specific problem is sufficiently robust (not context-dependent) and somehow well understood (causality), and if there are specialized (often emergent) supporting institutions devoted to research and teaching around these aspects, we claim that these are powerful signals of promisingness in order to bet on that technology.

2. The *standardized technical core* rule (R2): The possibilities for developing a technology to fix a problem increase when the technical core of a certain technology is sufficiently standardized in (rather) stabilized versions of the technology (prototypes, devices). Moreover, if there are (at least preliminary versions of) organizational forms suitable for the implementation and potential improvement of this technical core, then we claim that these are significant sources of promisingness for the specific technology.

3. The *enlightening testability* rule (R3): A technology is expected to advance smoothly when there are relatively sharp and uncontroversial criteria to detect improvements (in online practice, offline testing). Again, these criteria, together with the possibility of accommodating the enlightening testability methods in (at least tentative) organizational or institutional settings, constitute remarkable signals of potential advance along the concrete technological path.

4.2 Technological Advance, Supporting Institutions and Growth

The next step is to propose a stylized model in which we represent, as neatly as possible, two distinct realms (populations) of locations/agents of technical practice and a realm (population at a different layer) of spots/institutions bringing about new understandings, in coevolution. They coevolve on the basis of the mechanisms presented in Section 4.1 including formal versions of the rules R1, R2 and R3.

For simplicity, we will analyze the coevolution between two productive sectors and a population of scientific centers that carry out research and compete for funding and/or political support regarding their activity. The evolution of sectors (practice) feeds on the realm of scientific research; and, in turn, the evolving population of scientific centers feeds on the sectoral realms of technical practice. As is discussed in the first title in the Elements in Evolutionary Economics series (Lipsey 2018), different sources of dynamic increasing returns may appear in the process.

Let us define the set $I = \{1, 2, \ldots, n\}$ – with n a positive integer – as representing the set of spots/locations/agents of technical practice in Sector I, with $i \in I$ denoting the i-spot of technological practice within I. Likewise, let us denote by a_{it} the level of technological practice (labor productivity, perform-ance) in firm/organization i within sector I at time t, $t \in R$.

Besides this, we consider the existence of a different sector (another field of technical and productive activity) $J = \{1, 2, \ldots, m\}$, with m a positive integer and $j \in J$ being the j-firm/organization within sector J – or, in general, the spot j of technical practice in field J – whose level of technology at t is given by b_{jt}. Sets I and J could also be seen as different regions, within which we find competing locations (with regard to a specific field of activity) in such a way that these locations have heterogeneous technological-performance levels. Both regions would jointly conform to a nation or a concrete socioeconomic area. We can think of two economic areas/sectors/regions that provide alternative ways of doing something (producing energy and food; alternative ways of using chemical and physical procedures to cultivate and irrigate; transmitting infor-mation and transporting commodities and people).

For simplicity, we consider a constant level L of population in the whole economy that is divided in a permanent way among I and J. We then have constant corresponding shares of workers in each of the two sectors (because there are specific training skills or institutional conditions that impede the flow from one sector/region to the other; barriers to functional or geographical mobility; or legal frictions). With no loss of generality, we consider for illustrative purposes that each sector/region, I and J, employs 50 percent (each) of the overall population of workers.

In addition, we assume full employment and that there are no demand-side shortcomings or rationings in the output markets. Within each sector/region, we will denote by e_{it}, ε_{jt} the shares of sectoral/regional employment that work at time t in each firm/spot/location, $i \in I$ and $j \in J$. Therefore, $\sum_{i=1}^{n} e_{it} = 1$ and $\sum_{j=1}^{m} \varepsilon_{jt} = 1$.

In the model, we assume that the technology (labor productivity levels, performance) and the corresponding shares of labor are continuous and smooth functions of time. We also assume that production functions at the firm level are linear labor-technology functions in both sectors. This assumption could easily be removed (by considering capital goods) as we show in Fatas-Villafranca (2008, 2009).

Apart from the sectoral/regional populations I and J, we consider that there exists a third population, S, in the model – let us say, at a different layer, perhaps a supranational or international layer – that contains just two objects: We may think of two centers – research institutions and universities, two scientific fields materialized and embodied in specific institutional arrangements. More precisely, we define $S = \{A, B\}$, with A and B denoting different centers or agencies (spots/locations/institutions/agents) devoted to developing "new understandings" – public labs, universities, scientific associations. We suppose that these centers focus their activities in developing distinct supporting sciences related to the fields of technical practice that are evolving within I and J. Thus, the new understandings produced in $S = \{A, B\}$ are essential for generating advances in the technology used in sectors/regions I and J, respectively. More precisely, we assume that the advances in A are essential for I; and that the advances in B are essential for J.

Likewise, s_{At}, s_{Bt} represents the share of total scientific budget (or the share of resources of any kind) under the control of A and B, respectively, at any time, with $s_{At} + s_{Bt} = 1, \forall t$. We assume that both shares of budget/resources are continuous and differentiable functions of time. It is important to note that we also consider that s_{At}, s_{Bt} are proxies of the relative political support/funding/ promotion of A and B, respectively, in such a way that the higher the level of relative support s_{At}, or s_{Bt}, the stronger and more intense (relatively) the production of new understandings will be in the most benefited center/field/institution, A or B. For simplicity, we state that the flows of new useful understandings that A and B produce, respectively, during period t, are exactly s_{At}, s_{Bt}. Of course, we could incorporate here parameters or more sophisticated functional forms (see Fatas-Villafranca et al. 2009; Almudi et al. 2012, 2013).

We basically try to capture the idea that the higher the amount of funding/legal support/infrastructures allocated by society (public budget, policy-makers) to a certain field (represented in center A or in center B), the stronger the flow of new basic/supporting understandings (e.g. basic science) generated by said field; and we also want to represent the idea that these new understandings drive but at the same time depend on the relative performance of the correlative fields of technical practice (sectors/regions I and J).

As a concrete historical mention, we would like to suggest that the case studies in Camprubi (2014) highlight interregional and technological coevolutionary processes (qualitatively close to those we formalize here) operating in mid-twentieth-century Spain, which could be very significant for contemporary developing nations or economically emergent areas of the world. Given the conditions of the Spanish sociopolitical regime at that time, and the wide variety of technological advances involved (competing irrigation techniques, civil engineering, energy production in different parts of the country – central Spain vs. peripheral regions), all coevolving with institutional bodies at multiple layers (research institutes, professional associations, the state), this may be an enlightening historical study to apply our model in contemporary developing episodes (the Arab world, Latin America, Africa).

Thus, in what follows, and to complete our model, we incorporate the specific dynamic mechanisms underlying evolution and coevolution in the processes that we are figuring out. We draw on what we have stated in this section and on the models in Fatas-Villafranca et al. (2008, 2009, 2014) and Almudi et al. (2012, 2013) and we propose the specific intra-population (intra-sectoral/intra-regional) evolutionary flows that follow.

4.2.1 Assumptions on Intra-sectoral Dynamics

We now present sector/region-specific assumptions. Thus:

1. We assume linear labor-knowledge production technologies in firms/locations within sectors/regions I and J. Firms are profit-seekers that sell all they can produce (see Nelson and Winter 1982). The corresponding average (sectoral/regional) levels of technology (labor productivity) and the growth rates are:

$$a_t = \sum_{i=1}^{n} e_{it} a_{it}, \quad b_t = \sum_{j=1}^{m} \varepsilon_{jt} b_{jt} \tag{1}$$

and

$$\hat{a}_t \equiv \frac{\dot{a}}{a_t} = \frac{d}{dt} \ln a_t, \quad \hat{b}_t \equiv \frac{\dot{b}}{b_t} = \frac{d}{dt} \ln b_t$$

2. It is straightforward to show that, in an economy composed of two final
   sectors/regions, I and J, and in which both sectors maintain constant employment shares in the overall employed population (50 percent each), the
   overall rate of technological advance (or overall productivity growth) is
   given as:

$$\hat{q}_t = (1 + b_t/a_t)^{-1}\hat{a}_t + (1 + a_t/b_t)^{-1}\hat{b}_t \tag{2}$$

3. Firm i: innovation in Sector $I = \{1, 2, \ldots, n\}$. We consider that, for each
   $i \in I$, technology (labor productivity) grows depending on a cumulative
   effect (the previous level of practice) and on the scope (wideness) of the base
   of technological opportunities in the sector as being developed by advances
   in the supporting science produced by the center/field A. A wide discussion
   on this assumption can be found in Almudi et al. (2013). Of course, we could
   bring out now subtle elements to formalize catalyst or blocking factors
   regarding firms' regional-specific absorptive capacity of new basic knowledge. We deal with these elements in next sections. Here, since we have
   posed that new understandings arise in A and B as flows directly engendered
   by the share of budget/support received by the corresponding center, and
   since we want to introduce coevolution in a smoother and neater way, we
   propose that:

$$\frac{d}{dt}\ln a_{it} = s_{At} \tag{3}$$

4. Firm j: innovation in Sector $J = \{1, 2, \ldots, m\}$. We consider that, for each
   $j \in J$, technology (labor productivity) grows depending on a cumulative
   effect and on the scope or wideness of technological opportunities being
   opened by advances in the supporting science produced in center B. Since
   we have posed that new understandings arise in A and B as a flow engendered by the share of budget received by the corresponding center, scientific
   field or university, we propose that:

$$\frac{d}{dt}\ln b_{jt} = s_{Bt} \tag{4}$$

5. Intra-sector $I = \{1, 2, \ldots, n\}$ selection: Operating within the population of
   heterogeneous firms/locations (spots of technological practice) represented
   in Sector/region I, we can assume different types of selection processes. In
   Fatas-Villafranca (2008) and Almudi et al. (2012), we have assumed
   demand–supply (price/performance) competition in the goods markets. In

Fatas-Villafranca (2009), we assumed uneven capital growth rates depending on different profit rates, as in Nelson and Winter (1982).

Here, for clarity, we want to recall a topic we handled in Fatas-Villafranca et al. (2014); we propose competition among firms in terms of firms being able to attract skilled workers depending on the firm's productivity (technology) level. The rationale stated in Fatas-Villafranca et al. (2014) was the relationship between firm-specific salary ≈ productivity a_{it} and, additionally, skilled workers' interest – within sector I – in developing their careers by trying to access technologically progressive firms. It is a labor market selection argument in which skilled workers randomly meet and share their experience of different firms; then, they apply to be hired by the most dynamic firms (more technologically advanced and productive firms offering higher salaries). Sectoral evolution operates through the labor market of highly skilled workers who gradually discover, apply to and try to work at more advanced firms.

Formally, we assume random matching among skilled workers in Sector I and a flow of revision of the labor place that gradually leads workers to attempt to be hired by technology progressive firms. If this is so, we can assume that workers employed in firms i and k within sector I meet with size-proportional probabilities (with a market-parameter α capturing the facilities for job-market learning and applications), so that probabilities of random meetings as proportional to employment shares may be $(\alpha e_{it} e_{kt})$, with $0 < \alpha < 1$. Furthermore, we may represent workers tending to change their employment toward better firms or regions (higher productivity/salaries, better working conditions) by $f_{ikt} = max\{(a_{it} - a_{kt}); 0\}$ – the switching flow of workers from firm k to firm i at any period of time; thus we have a revision protocol:

$$f_{ikt} - f_{kit} = (a_{it} - a_{kt})$$

If we take together the pairwise-random matchings proposed, and the revision protocol of learning, it follows that the share of workers located in $i \in I$ evolves driven by the following replicator dynamics system (Almudi et al. 2017):

$$\dot{e}_{it} = \alpha e_{it}(a_{it} - a_t), \quad 0 < \alpha < 1 \tag{5}$$

6. Intra-sector $J = \{1, 2, \ldots, m\}$ selection: Within the population of heterogeneous firms or spots of technological practice in sector J, we can assume a similar argument. If, for the sake of simplicity, we assume the same value for

the market-learning parameter α, we can arrive at a replicator dynamics system driving competition within sector J:

$$\dot{\varepsilon}_{jt} = \alpha \varepsilon_{jt}(b_{jt} - b_t), \quad 0 < \alpha < 1 \tag{6}$$

4.2.2 Coevolution and Economic Growth

We close the model with the assumptions related to the realm of centers/institutions producing new understandings ($S = \{A, B\}$), which control and manage, respectively, shares of budget and support s_{At}, s_{Bt}, with $s_{At} + s_{Bt} = 1, \forall t$. These centers produce new applied and basic science that widen the technological bases of sectors I and J, respectively. In this bidimensional case, it is clear that $s_{Bt} = 1 - s_{At}$.

We now turn to consider a relative-fitness approach in this institutional layer of the model. Thus, we consider $g_B = 1$ as being the normalized fitness (in terms of the flow or generation of new knowledge) of center/institution B, with $g_A = (1 + a_t/b_t)$ being the relative fitness of center A. Notice that we are considering that center/field A is incorporating something clearly superior from a scientific and operational point of view (e.g. organic chemistry vs. knowledge on natural techniques to produce dyes), so that the relative fitness in A is identified as superior to g_B .

We will relax this assumption of clear perception in equation (13). Suffice it to note that it may be related to the principles condensed in rules R1, R2 and R3 (Sarewitz and Nelson, 2008b) regarding the maturity and clarity of understandings within a field as related to another, the existence of stabilized versions of the technology and enlightening testing methods that allow firms/locations in sector/region I to detect and control the superior relative fitness of A, thus having the possibility of dominating in technological progress over firms/locations in sector/region J (fed by B).

Let us note that we are assuming that the higher the level of technological advance in sector I (the one that benefits from advances in A) with respect to the technical level in J, – that is, the higher the ratio (a_t/b_t) – the higher the relative fitness of scientific institution A with respect to B. We introduce in this manner the role of advances in practice (by innovative firms testing the viability of certain theories, sharpening prototypes, lobbying on behalf of their supporting scientific field) in fostering and adding to the generation of new understandings (in their domain-related field of science or university system).

To simplify the math, we propose a simple bidimensional replicator, following Metcalfe (1998), according to which the center with higher-than-average relative fitness – which will be higher the greater the value (a_t/b_t) dependent on the evolution of sectoral practice – captures increasing shares of resources (budget) and political/social support and, in turn, generates more intense flows of basic/applied knowledge and understandings useful for its related field of practice. That is to say, eventually, the process will feed back into sectors.

Formally, since $s_{Bt} = 1 - s_{At}$ we are going to concentrate on the analysis of s_{At} by stating the following differential equation that captures all the reflections defined in 4.2.1

$$\dot{s}_A = s_{At}[g_{At} - (s_{At}g_{At} + s_{Bt}g_{Bt})] = s_{At}(1 - s_{At})\left(\frac{a_t}{b_t}\right) \tag{7}$$

Note that equations (1)–(7) fully drive the dynamics of our coevolution model.

As shown in the Proposition 4.1 (which conveys the first bundle of implications we obtain from this model), the evolving realms of technological practice *I* and *J* coevolve with (and through) the realm of institutions providing understandings, (*S*). The proposition shows interesting properties of this coevolutionary process between practice and understanding in its smooth variant.

Proposition 4.1

From equations (1) to (7) in the model, if we observe the coevolving dynamics in the three populations *I*, *J* and *S*, we can prove (separately) the following results ($V(a)_t$ and $V(b)_t$ are the variances in firm technologies within sectors/regions *I* and *J*, respectively):

1. The instantaneous rate of technological change (or rate of average productivity growth) in sector/region/realm of practice *I* is given by:

$$\hat{a}_t = \alpha\frac{V(a)_t}{a_t} + s_{At} \tag{8}$$

2. The instantaneous rate of technological change in sector/region/realm of practice *J* is given by:

$$\hat{b}_t = \alpha\frac{V(b)_t}{b_t} + 1 - s_{At} \tag{9}$$

3. The overall rate of technological change (overall rate of productivity growth in technical practice) is given by:

$$\hat{q}_t = \left(\frac{1}{1 + b_t/a_t}\right)\left(\alpha\frac{V(a)_t}{a_t} + s_{At}\right) + \left(\frac{1}{1 + a_t/b_t}\right)\left(\alpha\frac{V(b)_t}{b_t} + 1 - s_{At}\right) \tag{10}$$

4. Considering the results in items (1), (2) and (3), and keeping in mind that in our model we have $s_{Bt} = 1 - s_{At}$ the following dynamic path for the flow of new understandings in A closes the dynamic representation of our coevolution model:

$$s_{At} = \frac{1}{1 + \left(s_{A0}^{-1} - 1\right)\exp - \left(\frac{a_t}{b_t} \cdot t\right)} \qquad (11)$$

Proof

1. Drawing on equation (1) for a_t, if we take time derivatives and we consider equations (3) and (5), we obtain:

$$\dot{a} = \sum_i \dot{e}_i a_{it} + \sum_i e_{it}(a_{it}s_{At}) = \alpha \sum_i e_{it}a_{it}(a_{it} - a_t) + a_t s_{At} \rightarrow$$

$$\hat{a}_t = \alpha \frac{V(a)_t}{a_t} + s_{At}$$

2. Following exactly the same reasoning, departing from equation (1) for b_t and considering equations (2) and (6) in the time derivatives, we take the equation $s_{Bt} = 1 - s_{At}$ and we obtain $\hat{b}_t = \alpha \frac{V(b)_t}{b_t} + 1 - s_{At}$.

3. We consider equation (2) and we substitute equations (8) and (9). This gives us equation (10).

4. Equation (7) can be written: $\dot{s}_A = \left(\frac{a_t}{b_t}\right)s_{At}(1 - s_{At})$.

   Notice that this is a logistic differential equation with coefficient $\left(\frac{a_t}{b_t}\right)$.

   This differential equation can be integrated, leading (after standard changes) to an explicit solution for s_{A0} (as initial condition) which is the one presented in equation (11).

The four results presented in Proposition 4.1 convey ideal conditions for smooth coevolution driving technological progress in the model. They have been obtained in ideal conditions regarding (equal and maximum) firm-level absorptive capacity of relevant new understandings arriving at both sectors I and J, from centers A and B, respectively; we obtain the results assuming perfect observability of technological advances and understandings in both layers of the model: sectors I and J and population S. Thus, if we observe the results in Proposition 4.1, we obtain that in these ideal coevolutionary conditions:

$$\lim_{t \to \infty} s_{At} = 1,$$

(full support to the superior body of understanding A in the limit), with a speed given by the relative improvement in technical practice in the related field of practice I as compared with the other $\left(\frac{a_t}{b_t}\right)$; in turn, closing the coevolution argument, we see how s_{At} affects in opposite directions technical practice in I and J (see equations (8) and (9); see also equation (10)).

In fact, as intra-replicators equations (2), (3) cum (5) and (6) develop in "ideal" conditions, selection ends up concentrating activity in the frontier-level of activity in both sectors I and J, so that, in the limit, the variances tend to vanish and productivity stabilizes in sector J at a high level but it keeps growing in (the technologically superior) sector I, at a rate that fully feeds the limit trajectory of aggregate productivity growth $\hat{q}$.

In the specific setting of Proposition 4.1, coevolution operates without blockages in the direction of superior improvement potential, intra-population selections works relatively smoothly and feeds back in the "right" direction the production of new understanding. This dynamic path resembles a catalytic-type of process. This situation leads to a maximum performance in terms of long-run overall productivity growth (equation (10)).

It is interesting to see how these results get "worse" when we incorporate "imperfections" and possible obstacles in coevolution. Thus, let us focus on the mutualistic effect linking sector I and center A in the population of centers S and consider the following variations on the basic assumptions (we leave population J and its working mechanisms with no changes):

1. Let us now assume that firm-level absorptive capacity and the strength and propelling role of science produced in A is not equally distributed at top levels across sector I, so that we change equation (3) to equation (12) (where firm-specific parameter λ_i is a blocking factor in the operative assimilation of cause–effect scientific understandings and supporting science to develop practice):

$$\frac{d}{dt} ln a_{it} = \lambda_i s_{At}, \qquad 0 < \lambda_i < 1 \tag{12}$$

2. Let us consider that, even if the new understandings being produced in center A are potentially superior to those in B, the perception of the relative fitness may be imperfect (as measured by an opacity parameter $0 < \gamma < 1$ in the population dynamics within S) because of a lack of standardized technical cores to test the understandings and advance or because of a lack of enlightening testability methods (Sarewitz and Nelson (2008a) and Almudi et al. (2016) or rules R1, R2 and R3). The simplest way to introduce this change in the model is by reformulating equation (7) as:

$$\dot{s}_A = s_{At}[g_{At} - (s_{At}g_{At} + s_{Bt}g_{Bt})], \quad g_{At} = \gamma(1 + a_t/b_t), \quad g_{Bt} = 1 \tag{13}$$

With this formulation, equation (11) now becomes:

$$s_{At} = \frac{1}{1 + \left(s_{A0}^{-1} - 1\right)\exp\left(1 - \gamma(1 + a_t/b_t)\right)\cdot t}, s_{Bt} = 1 - s_{At} \tag{14}$$

We now must reformulate some of the previous results obtained in Proposition 4.1. Therefore, we present the new results in Proposition 4.2. As we will see, this new proposition reveals new aspects of coevolution.

Proposition 4.2 From equations (1), (2), (4), (5), (6), (12), (13) and (14), the new variant of the model, if we observe the coevolving dynamics in the three populations I, J and S, we can prove (separately) the following results:

1. The instantaneous rate of technological change (or rate of average productivity growth) in Sectors I and J are now given by:

$$\hat{a}_t = \alpha\frac{V(a)_t}{a_t} + s_{At}\left(\frac{C(a,\lambda)_t}{a_t} + \lambda_t\right) \tag{15}$$

$$\hat{b}_t = \alpha\frac{V(b)_t}{b_t} + 1 - s_{At} \tag{16}$$

2. The overall rate of technological change (overall rate of productivity growth in technical practice) is given by:

$$\hat{q}_t = \left(\frac{1}{1 + b_t/a_t}\right)\left(\alpha\frac{V(a)_t}{a_t} + s_{At}\left(\frac{C(a,\lambda)_t}{a_t} + \lambda_t\right)\right)$$
$$+ \left(\frac{1}{1 + a_t/b_t}\right)\left(\alpha\frac{V(b)_t}{b_t} + s_{Bt}\right) \tag{17}$$

3. Considering equations (13) and (14) and, keeping in mind that $s_{Bt} = 1 - s_{At}$, the following dynamic path for the flow of new understandings in A closes the dynamic representation of our coevolution model:

$$s_{At} = \frac{1}{1 + \left(s_{A0}^{-1} - 1\right)\exp\left(1 - \gamma(1 + a_t/b_t)\right)\cdot t} \tag{18}$$

Proof The proof is direct and straightforward if we follow the proof in Proposition 4.1 and we apply those procedures to the new variant of the model.

If we observe the results in Proposition 4.2, we perceive new aspects of coevolution. Thus, first, two very interesting terms appear now in the dynamics of technological change within population/sector I. These new factors are

$C(a, \lambda)_t$, which is the instantaneous covariance (across the sector I) between firm-specific technology levels and firms' absorptive capacity of new understandings (note that it can be negative, thus eroding sectoral progress); and λ_t, which measures the sectoral (over firms) average absorptive capacity of new understandings that come from center/field A and fuel sector I.

Second, attending to equation (18), we see that now the dynamic path of s_{At}, depends on the sign of $(1 - \gamma)\left(1 + \frac{a_t}{b_t}\right)$. This is is positive *iff* $\frac{a_t}{b_t} > \frac{1-\gamma}{\gamma}$, which means that the demonstration effect led by the standardized technical core rule and the testability of the new advances in practice (rules R2, R3) as given by $\frac{a_t}{b_t}$ must be sufficiently strong to beat and overcome opacity.

Of course, we are conscious that in such complex systems as those that coevolve in more complicated and realistic frameworks the role of the policy-maker becomes a highly problematic one. Thus, we believe that policy-makers, technology users and R&D investors need concrete strategies to approach decision-making in coevolutionary environments characterized by the difficulties exposed in Propositions 4.1 and 4.2 and even within more complex settings. This is the reason why, instead of extending the previous model, we prefer to devote a new subsection, Section 4.3, to tackling the issue of how to support policy-making, action and choice in innovative environments when coevolution is at work.

4.3 Innovation and Economic Catch-up

In this section, we draw on Sections 4.1 and 4.2 and propose a new approach to decision-making that may be of help for science and technology policy or for technology users and R&D investors in complex environments. In Section 4.3.1, we explore what should be done by policy-makers (decision-makers in general) to clear the stage and set the groundwork for technological advance before they address their processes of choice and action in complex frameworks. We use the concept of a *fuzzy set* to define, drawing on our results from Propositions 4.1 and 4.2, what we denote as the fuzzy set of promising technologies in a specific situation. Then, in Section 4.3.2, we use our previous results and this new concept to propose a formal *choice structure* that verifies interesting conditions as a decision-making procedure in complex environments.

4.3.1 Preliminaries for the Choice Structure

We explain here that the theory of fuzzy sets Zadeh (1965) provides us with interesting tools to support decision-making in ambiguous, unpredictable, and informationally poor environments. Fuzzy sets theory and aggregation methods can be of great help for R&D investment and for science and technology policy. These methods are suitable for mixing qualitatively different sources of information in radically uncertain environments, so that they are of great help for choice and policy decision-making in complex frames. Let us begin with some definitions.

Fuzzy set. Let X be a space of points, with a generic element of X denoted by x. Thus, $X = \{x\}$. A fuzzy set Z in X is characterized by a membership function $f_Z(x)$, which associates each point in X with a real number in the interval $[0, 1]$ with $f_Z(x)$ representing the "grade of membership" of x in Z.

Therefore, a fuzzy set is a class of objects with grades of membership between zero and one. The fuzzy set Z is often represented as $Z = \{X, f_Z(x)\}$.

In the specific case of technology policy or R&D investment, we can start by figuring out a situation in which public agencies, policy-makers or engineers within a firm must advance in trying to fix – with technology – a social or corporate problem P.

In the case of policy, if we want to relate this situation with the model explored in Propositions 4.1 and 4.2, we may think of the two sectors in that model as two industries aiming to improve a practice or to fix a problem through technology (the sector of production of lithium batteries or batteries in general, seeking to store energy at a large scale; and another sector involving firms aiming to develop superconducting magnetic devices to store energy, that is, seeking to fix the same problem; batteries uses electrochemistry as supporting science, and superconducting magnetic energy storage (SME) uses BSC-Theory). Policy-makers may try to assess the technological perspectives of alternative sectors in coevolution with their respective fields and institutions of understanding and then seek to allocate resources or to foster each of the sectors with certain intentionality.

Formally, we assume that the policy-maker (in general, decision-maker) faces (in order to solve problem P) a set $H = \{1, 2, \ldots, h\}$ of technological proposals (that still cannot fully solve the problem but are progressing through distinct paths), with h being a positive integer and $\tau \in H$ denoting a specific technological alternative in H.

Decision-makers or policy-makers can consult domain-specific experts regarding the degree to which each specific technology $\tau \in H$ verifies (giving a numerical equivalent between 0 and 1 – from null-fulfillment *to* full fulfillment) each one of the three rules R1, R2 and R3 highlighted in Section 4.1.2. We can denote by $p_{i\tau}$ the most frequent opinion, or the average, or median (between 0 and 1) among expert opinions, regarding the degree of verification of rule i ($i = 1, 2, 3$) by technology τ, at a time.

Let's define a set $\Phi = \{p_\tau\}_1^h$ with $p_\tau = (p_{1\tau}, p_{2\tau}, p_{3\tau})$ being the synthesis of expert opinions on the degree to which technology $\tau \in H$ verifies each of the rules R1, R2 and R3.

Set of promising technological paths. We can now define the fuzzy set of *promising technological paths* that may be under consideration to solve a specific social or corporate problem P. We define it as: $T = \{\Phi, f_T(p_\tau)\}$. The precise membership function $f_T(p_\tau)$ that we propose plays two roles: it combines the information in Φ; and it assigns accordingly, to each technology $\tau \in H$, a greater or lesser degree of membership to the fuzzy set T.

The literature on information fusion and fuzzy sets suggests certain convenient properties for the membership function $f_T : \Phi \rightarrow [0, 1]$ to be a nice aggregation operator. Thus, we are going to assume that f_T should verify the following properties:

1. Boundary: $f_T(0,0,0) = 0; : f_T[1,1,1] = 1$.
2. Monotonicity: If $\forall k, p_{k\tau} \geq p_{k\tau'} \Rightarrow f_T(p_\tau) \geq f_T(p_{\tau'})$.
3. Symmetry: $f_T(p_{i\tau}, p_{j\tau}, p_{k\tau},) = \bar{f}_T \epsilon [0, 1]$, no matter the order (i,j,k).
4. Absorbent element (veto): if $p_{j\tau} = 0$ for a $j, f_T(p_\tau) = 0$.
5. Neutral element: if $p_{j\tau} = 1$ for a $j, f_T(p_\tau) = f_T(p_\tau^{-j})$.

As we explain in Almudi et al. (2016), these properties can be interpreted according to economic aspects. The properties can be further developed and connected with alternative epistemic states of the decision-maker. Here, we suggest a specific functional form for f_T, which is as neat as possible, while still verifying properties (1) to (5). To be specific, the membership function we suggest is as follows:

$$f_T(p_\tau) = \prod_{i=1,2,3} p_{i\tau}, \ p_\tau = (p_{1\tau}, p_{2\tau}, p_{3\tau}), \ p_\tau \in \Phi, \tau \in H \qquad (19)$$

This function together with the aforementioned ideas allow us to define the fuzzy set of promising technologies as a tool to synthesize information and delineate the alternatives for the decision-maker. In the next part of this subsection, we propose a choice structure which allows decision-makers to operate in coevolutionary environments drawing on information synthesized by this procedure.

4.3.2 Learning, Development and the $\mathcal{T}$-Choice Structure

Let us state a *choice structure* $\mathcal{T} = \{\mathfrak{B}, C(\cdot)\}$ that consists of two elements:

1. A family $\mathfrak{B}$ of nonempty subsets of Φ. Every element (set) of $\mathfrak{B}$, that is, every $B \in \mathfrak{B}$, is a set $B \subset \Phi$ and it represents a specific institutional,

financial or technology-choice situation that may be conceivable for the decision-maker. Thus, $\mathfrak{B}$ is a set of conceivable decision-making settings that may be posed to (or figured out by) the decision-maker, involving technological alternatives seen as institutionally, financially or ethically co-feasible.

2. A choice rule $C(\cdot)$ which, formally, is a correspondence $C : \mathfrak{B} \rightrightarrows \wp(\Phi)$, (with $\wp(\Phi)$ denoting the power set of Φ), which assigns to every $B \in \mathfrak{B}$, a subset $C(B) \subset B$, such that $\forall p_\tau \in C(B)$ it is verified that $f_T(p_\tau) \geq \bar{f}$, with $\bar{f} > 0$ being a concrete technical threshold fixed by the policy-maker (decision-maker). Note that $f_T(p_\tau)$ is the function defined in equation (19)

The choice structure $\mathcal{T} = \{\mathfrak{B}, C(\cdot)\}$ is clearly inspired by the discussion presented in Section 4. The formal coevolutionary analysis and the discussion of rules R1, R2 and R3 have led us to the fuzzy set of promising technologies and opened the possibility of figuring out a choice structure that captures the combined roles of rules R1, R2 and R3 as coevolution catalysts or blocking factors, as mentioned in Section 4.1.2. The choice structure $\mathcal{T} = \{\mathfrak{B}, C(\cdot)\}$ moves one step further, since it considers the possibility of mutually exclusive alternative scenarios in terms of compatibility/incompatibility of technological supporting infrastructures to be built up, or financially/institutionally co-feasible technological alternatives. In addition, it states a rule for choice. Of course, $\mathcal{T} = \{\mathfrak{B}, C(\cdot)\}$ should be conceived as a choice structure that must be updated from time to time, as long as the coevolutionary mechanisms driving technological change may be transformed.

Note that the choice structure that we propose $\mathcal{T} = \{\mathfrak{B}, C(\cdot)\}$ is not a fully rational process of choice. It is much closer to the procedures for boundedly rational decision-making introduced by Simon (1955, 1957). Nevertheless, we show in Proposition 4.3 that $\mathcal{T} = \{\mathfrak{B}, C(\cdot)\}$ verifies the weak axiom of revealed preference (WA) as a minimum consistency requirement for choice. Afterwards, we will propose a correlative $\mathcal{T}$- index that is suitable for domain-specific applications in real cases.

Proposition 4.3 The $\mathcal{T}$- choice structure verifies the weak axiom of revealed preference (WA); but this is not equivalent to stating that $\{\mathfrak{B}, C(\cdot)\}$ is a standard structure of rational choice.

Proof Considering the way in which we have defined $C(B)$ in Section 4.3.2 (point 2), it is straightforward to verify that, if for some $B \in \mathfrak{B}$, with $p_\tau, p_{\tau'} \in B$, we have or we see that $p_\tau \in C(B)$, then for any $B' \in \mathfrak{B}$ with $p_\tau, p_{\tau'} \in B'$ and $p_{\tau'} \in C(B')$, we must have $p_\tau \in C(B')$. The monotone continuously increasing character of $f_T(p_\tau)$ in equation (19) and the role of this function in $C(B)$ assure this result. On the other hand, notice that, in general, since $\mathfrak{B}$ does not always include all the subsets of Φ of up to three elements, then we cannot rationalize the choice rule $C(B)$ relative to the family of sets $\mathfrak{B}$. Therefore, our suggested choice structure is not similar nor analogous to a process of rational choice

The weak axiom of revealed preference is a minimum consistency condition for our choice structure. It reveals proclivity to choose the same options in comparable situations and it eliminates the possibility of making contradictory fully irrational choices. We believe that this is a convenient requirement for a choice procedure; therefore, we are going to use the function $f_T(p_\tau)$ as shown in equation (19), the same function involved in the definition of $\{\mathfrak{B}, C(\cdot)\}$, as a statistical index for real use. This is the extension that we develop in the rest of this section. Thus, we suggest as a possible index $\mathcal{T}$ of technological promising-ness:

$$\mathcal{T}(\tau) = \prod_{i=1,2,3} p_{i\tau}, \ p_\tau = (p_{1\tau}, p_{2\tau}, p_{3\tau}), \ p_\tau \in \Phi, \tau \in H \qquad (20)$$

This index can be used in a domain-specific manner to explore and evaluate the characteristics of some of the alternative technologies aiming to fix a social or corporate problem.

More precisely, drawing on expert opinions, we can calculate this index for the alternative technologies $\tau \in H$ for problem P. In concrete applications, we may delineate the conceivable settings of choice (considering institutional, budget constraints) included in $\mathfrak{B}$ and then, after having fixed $\bar{f}$, we will choose [by applying $\{\mathfrak{B}, C(\cdot)\}$] a set of parallel efforts. This result could guide policy until the revision of the process in the future or it may be of help to bet on certain corporate paths. Let us note that, as compared with the indexes that we propose in Almudi et al. (2016), our new $\mathcal{T}$-index extracted from $\{\mathfrak{B}, C(\cdot)\}$ verifies exactly the same basic aggregation properties (see (1) to (5) in Section 4.3.1). What is new is that the index in this Element is neater than the indexes in Almudi et al. (2016).

Finally, in order to close this section, let us simply indicate that the application of equation (20) may also be of great help in guiding efforts to converge with leading nations on the part of developing countries. Thus, drawing on historical evidence and on a formal evolutionary model that we proposed in Almudi et al. (2012), we have delineated in previous contributions a stylized process of catch-up based on the conception of development as a learning process. The *stylized process of development and catch-up* synthesized in Almudi et al. (2012) has six features:

1. New emergent firms with clear national identities enjoy an initial advantage in prices in specific fast-growing technologically dynamic sectors. These firms from emergent nations must manage the transformation into techno-logical challengers to previous leaders during the process. Think of micro-electronics, computers, smartphones, logistic services, robotics and the corresponding competitive internationalized firms from Japan, Korea, China, India, Latin American nations and Israel.

2. For technological convergence to take place, it is essential that emergent developing nations can count on support from scientific institutions allowing for the absorption of worldwide frontier technology.

3. If these science-related institutions exist, the emergent nations and firms may benefit from the advantage of backwardness, even enjoying a high R&D efficiency through knowledge absorption.

4. If emergent firms eventually increase their R&D budget, then a gradual convergence in salaries can take place.

5. Institutional efforts to build up domestic high education locations and universities must occur; but then, there is the need (on the part of govern-ments) to make choices regarding strategic areas to be fostered.

6. Emergent firms and nations should be able to avoid insolvency problems that appear in the convergence process. All the six points and the sensitivity of successful catch-up to different sources of industrial convergence are stud-ied in Almudi et al. (2012).

The coevolution model in Section 4.2 indicates that these sources of advance are not obvious; they must be detected, decided on and implemented. In this sense, the $\mathcal{T}$-index extracted from $\{\mathfrak{B}, C(\cdot)\}$ can be useful in evaluating the technological promising-ness of alternative technological and institutional paths to support points 1 to 6. The concrete application of index in equation (20) that we suggest (regarding the stylized process of catch-up in Almudi et al. 2012) would consist of scanning the technologies and the coevolution aspects of technologies and institutions involved in enlisting points 1 to 6 through the calculation and evaluation of equation (20). In Almudi et al. (2016), we implemented the systematic procedure synthesized in the new $\mathcal{T}$-index extracted from $\{\mathfrak{B}, C(\cdot)\}$ to the evaluation of alternative solutions for the energy storage problem. This pattern of application together with the sensitivity analysis presented in Almudi et al. (2012) represents in our opinion a compact new approach to development policy that could be applied to contemporary national experiences. Of course, the coevolution concept we are developing in this Element plays a central role in this approach. Clearly, a wide range of potential applications can be explored in future research. For now, however, and considering the synthetic set of aims and the scope of this Element, in Section 5 we move on to a new application of the coevolution approach. We deal with a new set of political economy issues from our coevolution perspective.

5 Capitalism and Democracy in Coevolution

5.1 The Increase in Living Standards and Public Opinion

The potential relations linking capitalism and democracy have been a classic and very controversial issue in contemporary economic theory, at least since the work by Schumpeter (1942). The existence of a positive or negative (or even null) correlation between democracy, the development of market economies and rising living standards is still an open issue. We believe that this debate can be addressed from a new frame, in which the notion of coevolution and the discussions about the positive vs. negative collateral effects of technology-driven growth may be combined. As we show in Fatas-Villafranca et al. (2012), disruptive processes involving large and pervasive innovations generate (transitory) slumps of dynamism, slowdowns in productivity growth (in the mid-run) and institutional instability. The overwhelming long-run power of Schumpeterian creative destruction often generates unemployment in traditional activities and damaged regions, the destruction of parts of the economy and a worsening in income distribution in the short run. In contemporary capitalist-democratic societies, in which – at least in principle – the dynamics of public opinion should be materialized in the debate of free citizens and the institutional competition among alternative proposals on how to organize society, the political economy of emerging majorities and the dynamics of political power can be "irritating" evolutionary companions of innovation-driven economic growth. Moreover, the role of democracy in assuring innovative socioeconomic change has traditionally been a source of controversy that we now discuss.

Ever since the outset of contemporary theories in democracy, scholars and politicians (think of James Madison, Alexander Hamilton or Tocqueville) have had doubts regarding the capacity of citizens and public opinion as a whole to achieve a clear position on policy issues and aspects of economic change. There have always existed discrepancies between those arguing in favor of citizen judicious opinions (Dewey 1927) and those questioning the efficiency with which citizens can form an opinion (Lippmann 1922). Nowadays, and mostly considering the rich, complex and confusing information and communications technologies (ICT) environment in which citizens operate, political theorists agree that citizens' political knowledge is very superficial (Lupia, McCubbins and Popkin 2000). However, although it may seem paradoxical, considering citizen limitations, the second half of the twentieth century was a period in which democratic ideals were extended across the globe, and there are good reasons to state that, at least in the so-called mature democracies, citizens' political preferences have had an influence on the political and economic reality (Shapiro and Jacobs 1989). Stimson (1991) and Page and Shapiro (1992) have concluded that perhaps political ignorance at the level of individuals may transform into political collective wisdom when we observe public opinion dynamics as an aggregate entity. The problem with this argument is that it does not rely on any neat theory of how citizens come up with their opinions in complex evolving contexts.

In what follows, we consider the studies by Denzau and North (2000), Kahneman (2003) and Weidlich (2006), and we devise a coevolutionary argument suitable for tackling these issues. Moreover, we propose a framework that also incorporates recent contributions to evolutionary political economy (Muñoz et al. 2011; Hodgson 2015; Urmetzer et al. 2018; Novak 2018; Markey-Towler 2019; Van den Bergh et al. 2019). We present a coevolutionary formulation of the political economy problem that integrates the political side of economic agents not just as voters (as in public choice) but rather as competitive active agents (*citizens*) who try to bring about their conception of a good society and try to do this by supporting, and promoting their specific social *utopia* and the corresponding institutions.

We define a social utopia as an integrated set of ideas, values and vaguely envisioned institutions involving more or less efficient/innovative ways of producing and trading goods and services; equity standards; the role of traditions or cultural traits; the role of specific institutions – family, money, the nation state; and the perceived limits of nature. We consider that, in contemporary societies, there is a finite set of *utopias* that compete for social prominence and power. Drawing on Montgomery and Chirot (2015) and Almudi et al. (2017), we state that these social utopias (subsystems of citizens with a common view) comprise:

1. A cultural/traditional/ethno-nationalistic subsystem (looking for the prevalence of tradition-cultural related ideals and values).
2. A market subsystem (prominence of instituted classic-liberal or neoliberal values).
3. A civil society subsystem (libertarian and self-managed values that often move around a guiding ideal related to "more freedom" in some sense: civil rights, different varieties of anarchism, freedom to definitely transcend and transform the current definition of "conventional and standard" in specific realms).

4. A state subsystem (prevalence of centralist and communal property values organized around and ideal of a central state).

5. An environmental subsystem (preference for ecological or conservationist values).

In the coevolutionary model that we propose, the *citizen* chooses one of these subsystems as their utopia, a desired view of the world and a preferred organization of society – institutions and law in which one subsystem (their *subsystem*) dominates the other subsystems. This particular set of five is somewhat arbitrary. What is important is that our economic actor/citizen is affected by the coexistence of the subsystems in a certain relation of power and, as a citizen, they seek to promote one of these subsystems in preference to others. The result of this process of political competition is determined by (and it determines) coevolution within a socioeconomic institutional frame.

As we will see, competitive citizenship in our model affects the internal and inter-systemic evolution of subsystems, thus shaping economic payoffs. In turn, citizens can revise their degrees of contribution and can even change the utopia they support. In this way, they influence the relative size, power and presence of different worldviews and related institutions in the global socioeconomic system. Overall systemic evolution reshapes citizen payoffs, engendering new changes in choices and behavioral patterns and so on. In the following subsection we formalize these ideas.

5.2 Utopia Competition As a Coevolutionary Process

A society is composed of individual citizens who are boundedly rational economic agents. Likewise, the whole society can be decomposed into what we call *subsystems* that are formed by agents-citizens. As it has been described in Section 5.1, each subsystem represents a utopia.

Specifically, we consider five subsystems $\Pi = \{C, M, V, S, E\}$:

(C) cultural-traditional subsystem (prevalence of cultural/nationalistic values)
(M) free-market subsystem (classic-liberal or neoliberal values)
(V) civil society subsystem (libertarian and self-managed values)
(S) state subsystem (prevalence of centralist and communal property values)
(E) environmental subsystem (e.g. conservationist values).

An economic agent – who is also a citizen – is characterized in our model by their degree of citizenship when promoting a specific subsystem/utopia. We represent this degree of citizenship by the *proportion* of his total amount of resources (from now on including money, time, ideas) devoted to fostering their desired utopia at time t. For simplicity, we shall consider that citizens may position themselves in low (x_1), medium (x_2) or high (x_3) levels of contribution, such that $0 < x_1 < x_2 < x_3 < 1$.

We can even assume that $0 < x_1 < \dots x_i(x_i = x_1 + a(i-1)) < 1, a > 0$ and (x_1, x_2, x_3) are identical in all subsystems. The total population of citizens in a subsystem (promoting the corresponding utopia) will be distributed among these (three) alternative behavioral patterns at any time. For each subsystem $\pi \in \Pi$ at time t, let s_{jt}^{π} be the share of citizens within subsystem π whose level of citizenship is x_j. Therefore, $0 \leq s_{jt}^{\pi} \leq 1$, and $\sum_j s_{jt}^{\pi} = 1$.

5.2.1 Citizen Payoff

We include gains and (implicitly) costs in what we call each citizen's payoff. This payoff depends on:

1. The level of individual citizenship (contribution), which is a good for the citizen although it bears opportunity costs.
2. The relative size of the citizen's favored subsystem.
3. A double-externality effect through which citizens assess their (satisfactory but costly) level of effort, with respect to that of their subsystem peers.

Regarding factor (1), we assume that the level of participation and commitment in pursuit of a utopia is a source of satisfaction for citizens. With respect to factor (2), it is clear that agents devote their resources and ideas to implementing and extending the utopia associated with their favored subsystem – for example, building up new organizations and institutions that support the utopia's ideals, appearing in the mass media, shaping other citizens' minds. When the favored utopia increases its relative size and presence in society (gaining supporters, building up proper power structures), this benefits the citizen. Regarding factor (3), we incorporate here the opportunity cost of citizenship into the citizen payoff and the perception of the preferred utopia as being in danger because of peers' low commitment. We suppose that citizens try to avoid their peers' free-riding, while they get satisfaction from those even more committed peers. Likewise, the perception of close peers as being committed to the utopia in a low level is also a source of dissatisfaction that may move citizens to change their behavior. The simplest way to capture these local effects is by adding a double-externality component to the citizen payoff, in such a way that citizens are only affected by those citizens that are either slightly more committed or less committed than themselves. We incorporate a parameter φ regulating the relative intensity of externalities (permeability to local intra-subsystem commitment). Formally, we can represent these three effects in the following payoff functions for citizens in subsystem $\pi \in \Pi$:

$$
\begin{aligned}
u_{1t}^{\pi} &= \left(\gamma_t^{\pi}(1-\varphi) + \varphi s_{2t}^{\pi}\right)x_1 \\
u_{2t}^{\pi} &= \left(\gamma_t^{\pi}(1-\varphi) + \varphi\left(s_{3t}^{\pi} - s_{1t}^{\pi}\right)\right)x_2 \\
u_{3t}^{\pi} &= \left(\gamma_t^{\pi}(1-\varphi) - \varphi s_{2t}^{\pi}\right)x_3
\end{aligned}
\tag{1}
$$

with γ_t^{π} being the share of subsystem $\pi \in \Pi$ (share of supporters in society), $0 \leq \gamma_t^{\pi} \leq 1$, $\sum_{\pi \in \Pi} \gamma_t^{\pi} = 1$, and parameter φ, $0 < \varphi < 1$ capturing the intensity of the externality effect (permeability to peers opinion). In addition, we can define the average level of citizenship within each subsystem as $x_t^{\pi} = \sum_j s_{jt}^{\pi} x_j$. The average payoff within each subsystem at any time is $u_t^{\pi} = \sum_j s_{jt}^{\pi} u_{jt}^{\pi}$. Finally, it is clear that, the average level of citizenship in society at time t will be $x_t = \sum_{\pi \in \Pi} \gamma_t^{\pi} x_t^{\pi}$.

5.2.2 Intra-subsystemic Evolution

We assume that heterogeneous and boundedly rational citizens coexist within each subsystem. Thus, citizens differ in their commitment levels and, as we have seen, they gain a specific payoff attached to this contribution level. Since they feel the gains and costs associated to their behavior, they revise their level of citizenship. We assume two simultaneous mechanisms of change: First, in those cases in which the current payoff turns out to be low as compared to alternative behaviors (those observed in subsystem peers), the citizens may update their levels of citizenship. Second, we consider a mutation component among the different behavioral patterns so that, at any time, there are always citizens that change from one behavior to other. This mechanism captures spontaneous or innovative opinion changes (Appendix B1).

All this generates a collective *intra-subsystemic dynamics* through which citizens adapt their contributions depending on their relative payoffs. This intra-subsystemic dynamics drive intra-utopian evolution. Intra-subsystem dynamics could be studied in isolation as an analytical representation of learning and payoff updating in an evolving (instead of coevolving) framework. Thus, as an example, in Appendix B2, we present a brief close-form analysis of the intra-subsystem dynamics that emerge from the model. The key idea from Appendices B1 and B2 (an idea that will appear below in the coevolutionary setting), is that the relative weight of permeability to externalities in the payoff function *vs* the perception of being effective in action, is crucial for the isolated intra-subsystem dynamics. When externalities are very strong, a persistence of diversity in degrees of contribution emerges.

On the contrary, if externalities do not affect the payoff in an intense manner, then a tendency to conform on a unique behavioral pattern emerge (Appendix B2). This intra-subsystem result is also valid within our enriched coevolutionary setting in Section 5.2.3, although it is one among other effects operating in the coevolution model.

Keeping all this in mind, we pose then *five* intra-dynamics for *five utopias in competition*, driven by five (replicator) systems of (three) differential equations each (Appendix B1) where the payoff function is equation (1). The intra-subsystem dynamics are then driven by equation (2) and the payoff functions in equation (1):

$$\dot{s}_{jt}^{\pi} = (1 - \mu)s_{jt}^{\pi}\left(u_{jt}^{\pi} - u_t^{\pi}\right) + \mu\left(\frac{1}{3} - s_{jt}^{\pi}\right) \forall j, \forall \pi \in \Pi. \tag{2}$$

Equations (1) and (2) define the intra-subsystem dynamics in the model and, in Section 5.2.3, we complete the formalization of the *coevolution of five utopias*. For simplicity, we assume in equation (2) that $\mu = 0$.

5.2.3 Inter-subsystemic Dynamics and Coevolution

It seems reasonable to suppose that those subsystems that engender stronger levels of citizenship in support for the corresponding utopias will end up gaining relative presence in society. This effect will take place as long as citizens can change their minds and change their utopias because of the influence of the relative frequency and visibility of other citizens' opinion, the related institutions and regulations that may emerge, mass media, social networks. In turn, the emergent uneven prevalence of the alternative utopias will enforce in a higher or lower level the payoff of their related individual citizens. Those citizens perceiving the relative success of their favored utopia will feel reinforced and favored in their behaviors and ideas. On the other hand, citizens that perceive how their utopias lose social prevalence may, eventually, change their minds. Apart from this mechanism, we may also consider the possibility of citizens changing their opinion because of uncontrollable reasons (sudden opinion changes). We present this possibility in equation (3), although for formal simplicity we analyze the case for $\mu = 0$.

Formally, we close our coevolution model by proposing a (replicator with mutations) system of five differential equations, coupled (in a bidirectional way) with the intra-subsystemic dynamic systems presented above (Hofbauer and Sigmund 1998; Almudi et al. 2017). This last evolving system for the subsystems' shares may be expressed as follows (see Appendix B1):

$$\gamma_t^\pi = (1 - \mu)\gamma_t^\pi \left(x_t^\pi - x_t\right) + \mu \left(\frac{1}{5} - \gamma_t^\pi\right) \quad \forall \pi \in \Pi \tag{3}$$

Recall that $x_t^\pi = \sum_j s_{jt}^\pi x_j$, and we will consider $\mu = 0$.

5.2.4 Emergent Properties

These coupled dynamic systems generate a coevolutionary pattern of transformation and social change. As a result of this process, several global emergent properties may appear. Thus, the relative social presence for each utopia will endogenously change. To analyze some emergent properties in this model, we proceed through an analytical strategy in which we combine partial close-form results and computational illustrations.

Thus, we can infer from the analysis in Appendix B2 that the relative weight of peer-externalities is a deciding factor for intra-subsystem dynamics. Let us present another possibility to detect this effect in the model. Note that the payoff for each level of contribution (equation (1)) can be written as follows (assuming three levels of contribution $j = 1,2,3$):

$$\begin{bmatrix} u_{1t}^\pi \\ u_{2t}^\pi \\ u_{3t}^\pi \end{bmatrix} = \left(\gamma_t^\pi (1 - \varphi) \begin{bmatrix} x_1 & x_1 & x_1 \\ x_2 & x_2 & x_2 \\ x_3 & x_3 & x_3 \end{bmatrix} + \varphi \begin{bmatrix} 0 & x_1 & 0 \\ -x_2 & 0 & x_2 \\ 0 & -x_3 & 0 \end{bmatrix} \right) \begin{bmatrix} s_{1t}^\pi \\ s_{2t}^\pi \\ s_{3t}^\pi \end{bmatrix}$$

Equation (2) could be interpreted as the replicator dynamics of a population evolutionary game where players are randomly paired to play a two-player, three-strategy game where the payoff matrix is:

$$\left(\gamma_t^\pi (1 - \varphi) \begin{bmatrix} x_1 & x_1 & x_1 \\ x_2 & x_2 & x_2 \\ x_3 & x_3 & x_3 \end{bmatrix} + \varphi \begin{bmatrix} 0 & x_1 & 0 \\ -x_2 & 0 & x_2 \\ 0 & -x_3 & 0 \end{bmatrix} \right)$$

Let us consider the extreme values of φ. For $\varphi = 0$, we have the following subgame (henceforth SG1, for subgame 1):

$$\gamma_t^\pi \begin{bmatrix} x_1 & x_1 & x_1 \\ x_2 & x_2 & x_2 \\ x_3 & x_3 & x_3 \end{bmatrix}$$

Given that $x_1 < x_2 < x_3$, strategy 3 is dominant and evolutionarily stable. Thus, the point $x_1 < x_2 < x_3$ is asymptotically stable and the system converges to it from any initial condition with $s_3 > 0$.

On the other side, for the other extreme value $\varphi = 1$, we have the following game (SG2, for subgame 2):

$$\begin{bmatrix} 0 & x_1 & 0 \\ -x_2 & 0 & x_2 \\ 0 & -x_3 & 0 \end{bmatrix}$$

Now, strategy 3 is weakly dominated by strategy 1. As we saw in Almudi et al. (2017), the resting points for this SG2 are:

1. All points in line $s_2 = 0$, *and* $(s_3 = 1 - s_1)$.
2. Point $s_2 = 1$. This point is unstable and invadable by strategy 1.

In terms of our model, when citizens (within their utopia) are purely partisans $\varphi = 0$ (with no attention to externalities), in such a way that they just care about the rise to prevalence of their utopian social view without paying too much attention to what their peers are doing, then (in isolated conditions) the said subsystem tends toward a maximum average degree of citizen contribution. On the contrary, with a complete permeability in peer externalities, then citizens perceive intensely opportunistic behaviors and mild peer commitment and the subsystem evolution becomes more complex (even fluctuating paths of revised contribution can emerge). This is fully in line with Appendix B2.

In the general case, we have seen that equation (2) can be seen as the replicator dynamics of a composition of SG1 and SG2, weighted by factors $\gamma_t^\pi(1 - \varphi)$ and φ respectively. The composition would be:

$$\left(\gamma_t^\pi(1 - \varphi) \begin{bmatrix} x_1 & x_1 & x_1 \\ x_2 & x_2 & x_2 \\ x_3 & x_3 & x_3 \end{bmatrix} + \varphi \begin{bmatrix} 0 & x_1 & 0 \\ -x_2 & 0 & x_2 \\ 0 & -x_3 & 0 \end{bmatrix} \right)$$

Clearly, we have a continuum of possibilities by mixing the subgames. Note that the (now endogenous) factor $\gamma_t^\pi(1 - \varphi)$ is very relevant. We can infer that the lower the value of φ in a subsystem, the higher the average level of commitment in the specific subsystem (see also Appendix B2). Nevertheless, in the coevolutionary setting in which we consider equations (1), (2) and (3) together, assuming $\varphi > 0$, a feature of this model is that the dynamics of subsystems with low share (low value of γ_t^π) are mostly driven by subgame SG2. Therefore, in such vanishing subsystems eventually strategy 1 becomes dominant and strategies 2 and 3 effectively disappear. Hence, the dynamic outcome is no longer clear.

On the other hand, for those utopias (subsystems) that eventually reach high values of γ_t^π, even with relatively low values of φ, the subgame SG1 may prevail and we should expect a high average level of intra-subsystem citizen commitment.

The combined dynamics of SG1 and SG2 mixed in the coevolution settings (equations (1), (2) and (3)) must be explored through computational methods. We leave aside the complete exploration of the model for future research but we invite the reader to proceed with us in a more or less heuristic manner. We would like to focus the coevolutionary analysis on the role of the permeability in peer's local externality as determined by the value of parameter φ. We sum up some the findings that we have pointed out above:

For Low values of φ

As pointed out in the previous paragraphs, for low values of φ, in utopias/subsystems with low share of social support, subgame SG2 may drive the dynamics, so eventually strategy 1 becomes dominant, and strategies 2 and 3 effectively disappear. Then, we expect low average citizen commitment in these subsystems and may erode even more the low social support of the utopia. Which particular subsystem(s) will end up with a significant share γ_t^{π}, will depend on initial conditions. Clearly, a high value of γ_t^{π}, and, particularly, a high value of $s_{3,t=0}^{\pi}$ will be essential. This will be a deciding factor in cases in which, for example, two utopias depart from very similar (almost identical) shares of social support in the population.

Increasing values of φ

If we consider higher parameter values for φ, the analysis of the subsystem(s) with significant share γ_t^{π} is more complicated, as both SG1 and SG2 influence strongly the dynamics. Therefore, we will show an interesting possibility under these conditions through a computational illustration. This illustration aims at highlighting the surprising effects that a higher or lower permeability in peers behavior may have on the emergent social dynamics that lead to the predominance of one utopia. As we will see, depending on the value of φ, we can observe the emergence of a well-accepted market economy or, on the (very) contrary, we can obtain a very fast (almost sudden) rise to leadership and consolidation of a socialist pro-state type of society.

In order to illustrate this interesting result, let us present a *computational illustration* of the model, departing from the following basic setting for all the parametric values and initial conditions:

$x_1 = 0.05, a = 0.1, \gamma_0^M = \gamma_0^S = 0.25, \quad \gamma_0^E = 0.1, \quad \gamma_0^C = \gamma_0^V = 0.2$, and the intra-subsystem initial distributions of citizen contribution (from low to medium to high) that follow:

Market (0.6, 0.1, 0.3); State (0.2, 0.35, 0.45); Environment (0.35, 0.3, 0.35); Culture/Traditional (0.3, 0.35, 0.35); Civic (0.45, 0.2, 0.35).

We see in this setting how, mostly, the market (M) and the state (S) utopias depart from a highly significant level of social support (0.25 each) but also the cultural/traditional (C); and the civic (V) utopias are significantly supported. Even the environmental subsystem departs from a significant 10% of social support. We consider that the intra-subsystem distributions of citizen commitment are different and we are going to move and play with the value of parameter φ in the model.

Firstly, we will run the model for a parametric value $\varphi = 0.5$, (a high value). Then, afterwards, we will run the model (with all the parameter values remaining constant) but fixing a low permeability to externalities, that is, a low value $\varphi = 0.1$.

Figure 8 depicts the dynamics of γ_t^π for the five utopias when $\varphi = 0.5$.

As we see in Figure 8, the market utopia ends up prevailing in society (we end up with a fully market-oriented society). Let us note that, during half of the process, the state utopia is supported by a high share of society (it is the dominant subsystem) until the market vision beats it.

The analysis of the intra-subsystem dynamics of the market (M) utopia that ends up prevailing in society is very enlightening. We present the intra-subsystem market dynamics (underlying Figure 8) in a new figure (Figure 9). In Figure 9, we show how although, initially, the share of pro-marketers with very low level of commitment is high 60 percent (60 percent of pro-market citizens are almost not committed to defending their utopia), eventually, the number of citizens supporting the market grows significantly. In fact, there is an interval in which almost 90 percent of pro-market citizens are very much committed. This happens because, given the high sensitivity of citizens to what their peers are doing, and considering that many of pro-market peers show very low

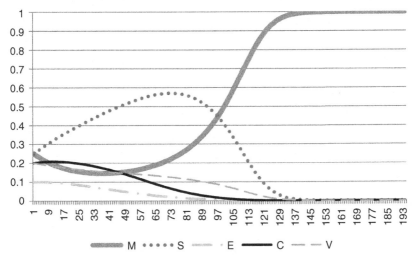

Figure 8 Utopia share in society γ_t^π (time evolution) ($\varphi = 0.5$)

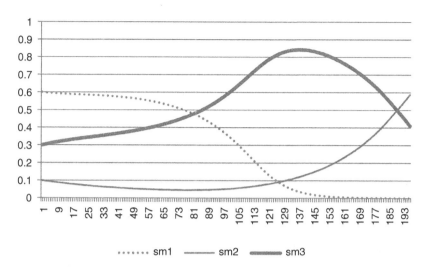

Figure 9 Market Utopia: Intra-subsystem evolution ($\varphi = 0.5$)

commitment levels, pro-market citizens with medium commitment levels (group sm2) become seriously concerned with the future of their envisioned social vision (consider jointly equations (1), (2), (3)). As can be seen in Figure 9, a strong flow out from mid-commitment (and even from low commitment) pro-marketers toward high commitment in pro-market citizens emerges. In Figure 9 (and keeping in mind what we have said in the formal analysis before), we see how a high permeability to the low commitment of a great share of one's peers moves many pro-market people to a strong defense of their utopia (which they see as potentially in danger). This process occurs with a high level of permeability ($\varphi = 0.5$, and it also happens for higher levels of this parameter). The permeability allows mid-committed pro-market citizens to discover and perceive that there are many low-level market supporters around them and that their social view is in danger. They then move to action for a while (high sm3). This is enough to lead the market vision to social dominance, as in Figure 8. As we can see in Figures 8 and 9, once the market vision seems to be assured, citizens soften their participation and move to a milder degree of involvement in social action (see the path of sm2; they devote resources to other activities).

It is now very interesting to analyze what happens if we assume a low level of permeability in what the citizen's peers are doing. Let us now fix a low level of parameter φ. We run the model for $\varphi = 0.1$, with everything else being equal.

As we see in Figure 10, the coevolutionary dynamics of utopia competition are now very different. The change in this parameter is enough for society to end up being centralized (perhaps socialist or communist). It is remarkable that the rise of the state utopia to dominance occurs in a very fast manner (Figure 10).

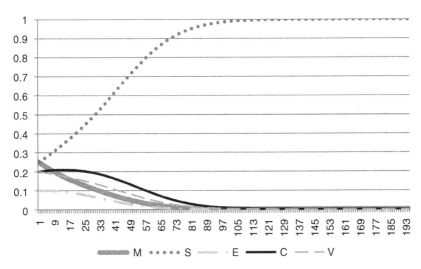

Figure 10 Utopia share in society γ_t^π (time evolution) ($\varphi = 0.1$)

If we analyze what happens now with the intra-subsystem dynamics under-lying Figure 10, we obtain Figure 11 (for the intra-market utopia evolution) and Figure 12 for the intra-state process of citizen commitment.

Figure 11 shows that the low level of permeability to what your peers are doing (note that within the market subsystem, as before, the initial level of very low-committed pro-market citizens is 60 percent, very high) leads to a very slow reaction of pro-market supporters. Initially the market utopia enjoys a nice level of social support (0.25 in the basic setting), and with a low level of φ, pro-markets do not worry much. They do not perceive the danger of many peers being reluctant to civic action. The process of moving to action is so slow and mild within the market utopia (compare Figure 11 with Figure 9) that the rise of the state utopia cannot be avoided.

If we look at the dynamics in Figure 12, we see how (initially) highly committed statist supporters who move on strongly overcome (this time) the mild and slow reaction of initially pro-market supporters. This is what is happening behind the aggregate picture in Figure 10. Let us note that, once the state utopia clearly begins to prevail, something akin to a *spiral of silence* process takes place within the market subsystem. By considering together Figures 10 and 11, we see that highly committed pro-market supporters (see the path for sm3 in Figure 11) eventually give up. Many of them turn away from high pro-market involvement when they perceive the strong rise of the state utopia to social leadership (see the decline of sm3 in Figure 11). Undoubtedly, this is a phenomenon that should make us think about the complex dynamics of

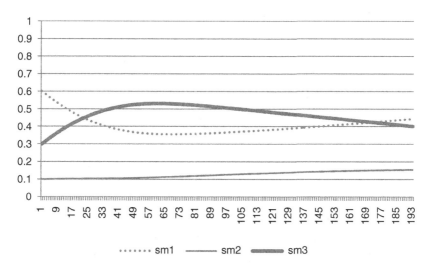

Figure 11 Market Utopïa: Intra-subsystem evolution ($\varphi = 0.1$)

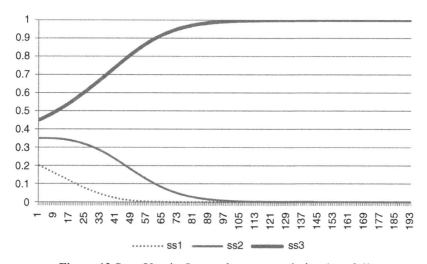

Figure 12 State Utopia: Intra-subsystem evolution ($\varphi = 0.1$)

sociopolitical trends in contemporary societies. We cannot explore the whole model in this single Element, but we pose some final reflections in Section 5.3.

5.3 The Dynamics of Power in Capitalistic Democracies

As we have seen, our coevolution model differs from the standard institutional approaches in that our frame is built around an agent of change – the economic actor as *citizen* who chooses a *utopia* that they seek to *promote* through their differential contributions. It is this citizen activity in our framework that causes the changes in the balance of subsystems/utopias (and so in the institutional structures) of a socioeconomic order. Reflecting on all the material presented in this Element, we would like to emphasize that it is very important to develop the *normative debate* within the realm of evolving complex systems (Pyka 2017). We believe that the coevolution approach is a perfect frame to tackle this open issue. As illustrative examples of open pieces for future reflection, we suggest that the coevolution approach can deal with the following problems:

1. In coevolutionary complex systems, it is a key issue detecting the origin and possible sudden accumulation of blocking factors, rationings and inefficiencies in action. Smooth coevolution is never assured and what is convenient for the common good seems always to be open to conflict.

2. It is necessary to monitor potential infection routes (through and across sub-realms) that may engender surprising institutional pathologies, social conflicts, big rips due to innovative structural change and the ongoing confrontation of incompatible societal visions. Furthermore, the disruptive consequences of large innovations may lead to a possible deterioration of social and natural cohabitation.

3. Finally, we believe that exploring the motivational sources underlying growth and innovative change, which often have unclear welfare effects and collateral implications, is an analytical need that should always be tackled when studying socioeconomic coevolutionary environments. Of course, an analysis of these problems goes far beyond the scope of the present work but we pose them herein as promising lines for future research.

6 Synthesis and the Road Ahead

In this Element, we have delineated a characterization of contemporary capitalist economies as systems formed by structurally distinct (but dynamically codetermined) realms that coevolve. We refer to coevolution in economic systems in the sense that certain domain-specific innovation, replication and selection mechanisms mutually shape each other across socioeconomic subsystems thus engendering price trajectories, evolving market paths, technological change, growth and more or less sustainable dynamics of political change. The resulting theoretical frames and analytical outcomes have revealed coevolutionary paths characterized by distinct potentials, viability conditions, possible blockages and policy needs.

Hopefully, the reader will have perceived possibilities for advancing toward an overarching framework in evolutionary economics in our approach. We believe that our coevolution approach facilitates the combination of insights from the evolutionary-naturalistic perspectives in economics, the powerful Schumpeterian models and even close subfields such as evolutionary game theory, computational economics, institutional economics and more individualistic approaches. Perhaps our proposal will help future scholars to recognize that the ontological approaches highlighting intentionality and creative individual behavior, the Darwinian (or non-Darwinian) naturalistic approaches to socioeconomic change, the institutional and strategic management analysis of firm behavior and the developments on Schumpeterian industry studies and growth, are not mutually exclusive but complementary.

Likewise, from a methodological perspective we have tried to show how alternative formal approaches can be fruitfully cross-fertilized within the coevolution frame. Thus, we have combined closed-form and computational methods in this Element; we have dealt in a complementary manner with replicator dynamics models and ABMs; and we have indicated lines of advance by incorporating complex coevolving networks in our theoretical frame. These three types of models are useful for incorporating the coevolution concept and their combined use could correct the recent trend to work on high-dimensional obscure models within the evolutionary stream.

Finally, we would like to mention two ideas. First, we have claimed that evolutionary economic theory can proceed nowadays without the need of becoming involved in scholastic para-biological debates. In our opinion, after four decades of intense work, we already have the pillars on which we can develop evolutionary economic theory for its own sake, without going further into biological analogies. Second, the seemingly complicated image of socioeconomic systems that emerges from the coevolutionary approach does not lead us to say that contemporary societies are out of control, irremediably imperfect and/or condemned to fail. This is not at all the lesson that we should extract from the preceding pages. On the contrary, evolutionary economics (and the coevolution approach as a new step in this line) serves to enrich our understanding and provides us with the tools to deal with complex economic systems. Nowadays, we have already traveled a fair part of the way and have learned a wide bundle of working mechanisms and policy strategies so that evolutionary economists can deal with real problems with certain guarantees of success. Of course, we need to make the effort to clarify and transmit in a more compact and systematic way the mechanisms and policies that we have already found. Nevertheless, we would like to finish this work with an optimistic assessment of the current state of evolutionary economics and with a plea for new models and formal theoretical work oriented to condense, explore and develop the insights we have already uncovered during the last four decades.

Appendix A

Coevolution in Markets: Evolutionary Microfoundations for Sector 2, a Formal Analysis and the Two-Sectors Model in Pseudocode

A1 Microfoundations for the Demand-Side of Sector 2

In this appendix, we briefly suggest a way to state evolutionary microfoundations for the replicator dynamics system posed in Section 3.1.3, equation (10). As we have seen in Section 3.1.3, we can normalize the size of Sector 2 to a constant size. Consumers may revise their consumption options as time passes, and they may change the firm that they buy from as they learn about the market. This process would drive the dynamics of market shares. For simplicity, we will focus on the case of Sector 2 having a constant number of firms n, with $i = 1, \ldots, n$. These firms offer distinct varieties of consumption goods with different qualities and prices (which we assume to be constant for simplicity). These dimensions may be combined (as in Section 3.1.3) in firm's competitiveness indicator $\alpha_2 \frac{y_i}{y^{max}} + (1 - \alpha_2)\left(1 - \frac{p^i}{p^{max}}\right)$. It is clear that the proportion of consumers demanding the variety supplied by firm i at any time t is denoted by $s_i(t)$. We now consider that the final consumers opting for each possible firm i get a consumer payoff denoted by (see Section 3.1.3):

$$u_i = \alpha_2 \frac{y_i}{y^{max}} + (1 - \alpha_2)\left(1 - \frac{p^i}{p^{max}}\right)$$

We suppose that consumers gradually try to discover better options (cheaper and/or superior-quality options) and then they may change the firm they buy from. More precisely, we propose that consumers meet in the market with a probability that is proportional to the share of consumers buying i or j at any time. Then, consumers meet with a probability that is proportional to the sizes of the existing groups of consumers: $\delta s_i s_j$, $0 < \delta < 1$. From these meetings consumers share information regarding their current consumption experiences, learn from the market situation and may revise their choices after having observed others. That is to say, consumers may decide to buy from a different firm.

We denote by f_{ij} the rate at which consumers buying from firm j switch to firm i, in their pursuit of more satisfactory consumption patterns. Let us consider that the net switching rate among firms is:

$$f_{ij} = \theta[u_i - u_j]_+ = \theta max(u_i - u_j; 0), \quad \theta > 0$$

where $\theta > 0$ captures the ease with which consumers revise their behavior. We are assuming that, by comparing the satisfaction u_i with the u_j enjoyable when buying to firm j, consumers may decide to change their behavior.

Thus, we have a certain flow of heterogeneous boundedly rational consumers gradually moving in the (endogenously changing, nonunique) "better-valuation" direction, as given by the distribution of payoffs:

$$u_i = \alpha_2 \frac{y_i}{y^{max}} + (1 - \alpha_2)\left(1 - \frac{p^i}{p^{max}}\right), \quad i = 1, \ldots, n.$$

We have stated that the product $\delta s_i s_j (0 < \delta < 1)$ gives the probability for a random and independent interaction between one consumer buying from i(share in the population s_i) and another buying from j (share s_j). Then in a small interval Δt the flow of consumers from j to i would be given by (see Hofbauer and Sigmund 1998):

$$\delta s_i s_j f_{ij} \Delta t$$

and the change in the proportion of consumers buying to firm i will be:

$$\Delta s_i = \sum_j \delta s_i s_j (f_{ij} - f_{ji}) \Delta t, \quad f_{ij} - f_{ji} = \theta(u_i - u_j)$$

In turn, the continuous time evolution of the proportion of consumers buying from firm i may be described by the following equation:

$$\frac{ds_i}{dt} = \sum_j \delta s_i s_j (f_{ij} - f_{ji}) = \delta s_i \sum_j s_j \theta(u_i - u_j), \quad \dot{s}_i = \theta \delta s_i \left(u_i - \sum_j s_j u_j\right)$$

or changing velocity ($i = 1, .., n$):

$$\dot{s}_i = s_i(u_i - \bar{u}), \quad \text{where } \bar{u} = \sum_j s_j u_j$$

In this way, we obtain an evolutionary micro-founded basis to think about the driving forces underlying equation (10) in Section 3.1.3.

Let us note that in our two-sector coevolution model in Section 3, the stochastic evolving network upstream (Sector 1) is continuously fueling

Sector 2 with new knowledge and new machine prices. This flow engenders changing distributions of the consumer satisfaction levels:

$$u_i = \alpha_2 \frac{y_i}{y^{max}} + (1 - \alpha_2)\left(1 - \frac{p^i}{p^{max}}\right), \quad (i = 1,.., n)$$

In turn, as this distribution of consumer payoffs and the corresponding distribution of market shares for firms in Sector 2 is updated, this process induces a new distribution of potential users and absorption intervals in the demand-side of Sector 1. Sector 1 and Sector 2 coevolve. We have a market selection process in Sector 2 represented by a replicator dynamics system that is fueled by ongoing novelty generated upstream (in Sector 1). Conversely, the replicator dynamics in Sector 2 generate new framing conditions for the network dynamics in Sector 1.

A2 A Formal Analysis for a Simplified Version of the Model

We present here the proof for Proposition 3.1 in Section 3.2.2 that analyzes the dynamics of the simplified system (equation 14). For the sake of ease, we remind the reader that equation (14) is given as:

$$\begin{aligned}\dot{s}_i &= \beta s_i(t)\left[\sum_{j=1}^{n} s_j(t)p_j(t) - p_i(t)\right] \\ p_i(t) &= 1 + \alpha_i s_i(t), \quad (i = 1, 2, \ldots, n)\end{aligned} \tag{14}$$

The dynamics of equation (14) develop on the unit-simplex Δ^n and both the boundary and the interior of Δ^n are invariant sets (Sandholm 2010). We will focus on the interior of the simplex $D = \text{Int}(\Delta^n)$, since we are interested in checking the existence and stability of possible interior resting points. Proposition 3.1 (and in Section 3.2.2) synthesize the key result:

Proposition 3.1 The general replicator system (14) has a unique interior equilibrium point $s^* \in D = \text{Int}(\Delta^n)$. This point s^* is globally asymptotically stable within D.

Proof

1. First, we find that there is always at least an interior resting point $s^* \in D = \text{Int}(\Delta^n)$ for equation (14), which is given by:

$$s^* = \left(s_1^*, s_2^*, \ldots, s_n^*\right) = \left(\frac{\alpha_2\alpha_3 \ldots \alpha_n}{\sum_i \frac{(\alpha_1\alpha_2 \ldots \alpha_n)}{\alpha_i}}, \frac{\alpha_1\alpha_3 \ldots \alpha_n}{\sum_i \frac{(\alpha_1\alpha_2 \ldots \alpha_n)}{\alpha_i}}, \ldots, \frac{\alpha_1\alpha_2 \ldots \alpha_{n-1}}{\sum_i \frac{(\alpha_1\alpha_2 \ldots \alpha_n)}{\alpha_i}}\right)$$

It is straightforward to see that, if we substitute this expression in equation (14), we obtain that in s^*, $\dot{s}_i = 0, \forall i$ is always verified.

2. Second, we have to check also the stability of s^*. In fact, since we are going to verify that s^* is globally asymptotically stable within D, we also see that s^* is the unique equilibrium within D. We proceed by using the direct Lyapunov method of proof (Weibull 1995). Thus, we have defined $D = Int(\Delta^n)$ which is an open invariant set, in fact it is an invariant neighborhood of the interior equilibrium point s^*. By using the Lyapunov method, we can assure that s^* is unique and globally asymptotically stable within D if we find a continuous and differentiable function $V : D \rightarrow R$ which verifies the following properties in D:

1. $V(s) = 0 \Leftrightarrow s = s^*$, and $V(s) > 0 \; \forall s \neq s^*$ in D.
2. $\forall s \neq s^*$ in D, and we also see that $\frac{dV(s)}{dt} < 0$

For our general system (equation (14)) and the pricing routine $p_i(t) = 1 + \alpha_i s_i$, we can prove that $V(s) = -\sum_{i=1}^{n} ln\left(\frac{p_i(t)}{\bar{p}(t)}\right) = -\sum_{i=1}^{n} ln\left(\frac{1+\alpha_i s_i(t)}{\sum_{i=1}^{n} s_i(t)(1+\alpha_i s_i(t))}\right)$ is a strict Lyapunov function in D, verifying conditions (1) and (2). Let us verify this:

Regarding (1), note that in s^* all prices are equal and identical to the average price $\bar{p}(t)$. As a consequence $V(s^*) = -\sum_{i=1}^{n} ln(1) = 0$.

On the other hand, for any $s \neq s^*$ within D, $V(s) = -\sum_{i=1}^{n} ln\left(\frac{p_i(t)}{\bar{p}(t)}\right) >$

$0 \Leftrightarrow \sum_{i=1}^{n} ln\left(\frac{p_i(t)}{\bar{p}(t)}\right) < 0 \Leftrightarrow ln\left[\prod_{i=1}^{n}\left(\frac{p_i(t)}{\bar{p}(t)}\right)\right] < 0 \Leftrightarrow e^{ln\left[\prod_{i=1}^{n}\left(\frac{p_i(t)}{\bar{p}(t)}\right)\right]} < e^0 (= 1)$.

It is clear that this is verified if and only if:

$$\prod_{i=1}^{n}\left(\frac{p_i(t)}{\bar{p}(t)}\right) < 1$$

This expression is equivalent to proving that $(p_1(t).p_2(t)....p_n(t)) < \bar{p}(t)^n$. Then, this expression is true if $\bar{p}(t) > \sqrt[n]{p_1(t).p_2(t)....p_n(t)}$. We remember that $\bar{p}(t)$ is the weighted average of the prices in the sector, while $\sqrt[n]{p_1(t).p_2(t)....p_n(t)}$ is the geometric mean of those prices. With all prices being positive, and considering a non-excessive degree of price dispersion (since we are modeling a sector in which close varieties of the same good are produced and supplied), then we can affirm that $\bar{p}(t)$ is a sufficiently good approximation of the arithmetic mean of the prices. Then, the arithmetic mean is always significantly higher than the geometric mean, and therefore, in our conditions, $\bar{p}(t) > \sqrt[n]{p_1(t).p_2(t)....p_n(t)}$ and condition 1) (for $V(s)$ to be a strict Lyapunov function) is verified. We can affirm that $V(s) = 0 \Leftrightarrow s = s^*$ and $V(s) > 0 \; \forall s \neq s^*$ in D.

Regarding (2), we need to verify first, as a previous step, that for the pricing routine $p_i(t) = 1 + \alpha_i s_i$ and system given by equation (14) it is $\frac{d\bar{p}}{dt} = \frac{d\left(\sum_{i=1}^{n} s_i(t) p_i(t)\right)}{dt} < 0$.

Notice that the average price with this routine is $\bar{p} = 1 + \sum s_i^2 \alpha_i$.

Considering equation (14) we take derivatives in $\bar{p}$:

$$\frac{d\bar{p}}{dt} = -2\beta \sum_{i=1}^{n} s_i(\alpha_i s_i)(p_i - \bar{p}) = -2\beta Cov(\alpha s, p) < 0$$

It is clear that this is true because, since $p_i(t) = 1 + \alpha_i s_i$, the covariance between the prices (p_i) and the margins $(\alpha_i s_i)$ is positive.

Therefore,

$$\frac{d\bar{p}}{dt} < 0$$

Now, by taking derivatives in $V(s)$ we obtain that:

$$\frac{dV(s)}{dt} = - \left[\sum_{i=1}^{n} \frac{\left(\frac{dp_i}{dt}\right)}{p_i} - n \frac{(d\bar{p}/dt)}{\bar{p}} \right]$$

We have to prove that this expression is negative in the domain. We know from the previous step (notice $\frac{d\bar{p}}{dt} < 0$) that $-n\frac{(d\bar{p}/dt)}{\bar{p}} > 0$, but we have to study the remaining summand.

That is to ask, what can we state regarding the sign of $\sum_{i=1}^{n} \frac{\left(\frac{dp_i}{dt}\right)}{p_i}$? From the system given by equation (14) and its pricing routine it is clear that:

$$\sum_{i=1}^{n} \frac{(dp_i/dt)}{p_i} = -\beta \sum_{i=1}^{n} s_i \left(\frac{\alpha_i}{p_i}\right)(p_i - \bar{p}) = -\beta Cov\left(\frac{\alpha}{p}, p\right) > 0$$

We can see that the expression is positive since we have a negative covariance between the prices (p) and something divided by the prices. Then, having found that in our conditions both $\sum_{i=1}^{n} \frac{(dp_i/dt)}{p_i} > 0$ and $-n\frac{(d\bar{p}/dt)}{\bar{p}} > 0$ we can affirm that:

$$\frac{dV(s)}{dt} < 0$$

Therefore, we have verified that a *strict Lyapunov function* exists with the expression:

$$V(s) = -\sum_{i=1}^{n} ln\left(\frac{p_i(t)}{\bar{p}(t)}\right) = -\sum_{i=1}^{n} ln\left(\frac{1 + \alpha_i s_i(t)}{\sum_{i=1}^{n} s_i(t)(1 + \alpha_i s_i(t))}\right) \text{ for equation (14).}$$

This finding assures with full generality that the point s^* is a unique and globally asymptotically stable resting point within $D = Int(\Delta^n)$.

A3 Parametric Values and the Model in Pseudocode

We use subscript i for any firm in Sector 1; j for firms in Sector 2; k otherwise.

Notation Regarding Sector 1

$C_{i,t}^1$: firm i from Sector 1 at t.
$S_t^1 = \{C_{i,t}^1\}$: set of firms operating in Sector 1 at t.

Parameters in Sector 1 and base-setting
$\alpha_1 = 0.5$ Performance/price sensitivity of demand
$\eta = 1.5$ Common parameter in pricing routine
$c = 0.01$ Unit production cost
$\phi = 0.5$ Relative importance imitation vs. inner R&D
$\varepsilon = 0.75$ Entry cost for new imitative entrants
$\lambda = 0.05$ Probability of entering doing innovation

Firm-specific parameters in Sector 1
$r_i \sim U(0,1)$ Share of profits devoted to R&D
$\sigma_i \sim U(0,1)$ Radius delimiting perceived direct competitors

Firm-specific variables Sector 1
$x_{i,t} \in [0,1]$ Technological level in relative terms
$q_{i,t}^e \geq 0$ Expected sales (in real terms = number of expected customers)
$R_{i,t} \geq 0$ R&D spending
$c_{i,t}^e > 0$ Expected total unit cost
$\mu_{i,t} > 1$ Unit profit mark-up on costs
$p_{i,t} > 0$ Price
$\gamma_{i,t} \in [0,1]$ Firm knowledge
$q_{it} > 0$ Sales (in real units = number of customers)
$s_{it} \in [0,1]$ Market share
$c_{i,t} > 0$ Total unit cost (ex post)
$\pi_{i,t} \geq 0$ Total firm profit

Notation Regarding Sector 2

$C_{j,t}^2$: firm j in Sector 2 at t.
$S_t^2 = \left\{ C_{j,t}^2 \right\}$: Set of firms in Sector 2 at t.

Parameters in Sector 2 and base-setting	
$\alpha_2 = 0.5$	Performance/price sensitivity of demand
$\lambda = 0.05$	Probability of entry doing innovation (equal in both sectors)
$\delta = 1.06$	Common parameter in pricing routine
$a = 1$	Parameter Beta distribution
$b = 1$	Parameter Beta distribution

Firm-specific parameter Sector 2	
$\rho_j \sim \text{Beta} (a, b)$	Cognitive absorptive capacity (as a radius)

Firm-specific variables in Sector 2	
$X_{j,t} \in [0, 1]$	Knowledge to manage machines
$c_{j,t} > 0$	Cost of the machine
$y_{j,t} \geq 0$	Machine quality
$p_{j,t} > 0$	Price of the variety of consumption good
$f_{j,t} \in [0, 1]$	Consumption good firm-specific fitness (quality/price)
$s_{j,t} \in [0, 1]$	Market Share
$\pi_{j,t} \geq 0$	Firm profit

Pseudocode (Algorithm)

1. Initialize:
   1.1. Sector 1 (machines production). Initially empty sector- ($S_0^1 = \varnothing$).
   1.2. Sector 2 (consumption goods). Initially empty sector- ($S_0^2 = \varnothing$).
   1.3. END;
2. For any t:
   2.1. Call Entry_Sector1;
   2.2. Call Entry_Sector2;
   2.3. Call Operate_Sector1;
   2.4. Call Operate_Sector2;
   2.5. Call Apply_Replicator_Sector1;

2.6. Call Apply_Replicator_Sector2;
2.7. Call Exit_Sector1;
2.8. Call Exit_Sector2;
2.9. END;
3. END;

➤ Define Entry_Sector1:

1. Entry Sector 1: One new firm i enters in Sector 1 $\left(S_t^1 = S_{t-1}^1 \cup \{C_{i,t}^1\}\right)$;
2. With probability λ, or if the sector is empty, then $S_t^1 = \{C_{i,t}^1\}$ random initialization of traits:

   $r_i \sim U(0,1)$;

   $\sigma_i \sim U(0,1)$;

   $x_{i,t} \sim U(0,m)$, $m = x_{t-1}^{max}$ if x_{t-1}^{max} exists, or $m = 1$ otherwise;

3. If the new entrant copies, then: it copies firm $k \neq i$, with probability proportional to market share, so that:

   $r_i = r_k$;
   $\sigma_i = \sigma_k$;
   $x_{i,t} = x_{k,t-1}$;

4. Normalize $\sum_i x_{i,t} = 1$. The new entrant affects sectoral technology levels;
5. END;

➤ Define Entry_Sector2:

1. Entry Sector 2: A new firm j enters Sector 2 $\left(S_t^2 = S_{t-1}^2 \cup \{C_{j,t}^2\}\right)$;
2. Recalculate market shares: $s_{j,t} = 0.005$, $\sum_k s_{k,t} = 1 - s_{j,t} = 0.995$;
3. With probability λ, or if the sector is empty, random initialization of traits:,

   $\rho_j \sim \text{Beta}(a,b)$;

   $x_{j,t} \sim U(0,m)$, $m = x_{t-1}^{max}$ if x_{t-1}^{max} exists, or $m = 1$ otherwise;

4. If the new entrant copies, then: It copies firm k in Sector 2, with a probability which is proportional to its market share and:

   $\rho_j = \rho_k$;

   $X_{j,t} = X_{k,t-1}$;

5. END;

➤ Define Operate_Sector1:

1. For each firm i in Sector 1:
    1.1. R&D Investment:
        1.1.1. If it is a new imitative entrant: $R_{i,t} = R_{k,t}$;
        1.1.2. otherwise: $R_{i,t} = r_i\pi_{i,t-1}$;
    1.2. Expected unit cost:
        1.2.1. If it is a new imitative entrant: $c_{i,t}^e = c + \varepsilon\frac{R_{i,t}}{q_{i,t}^e}$, $q_{i,t}^e = q_{k,t-1}$
        1.2.2. If it is a new entrant but it does not imitate: $c_{i,t}^e = c$;
        1.2.3. otherwise $c_{i,t}^e = c + \varepsilon\frac{R_{i,t}}{q_{i,t}^e}$, $q_{i,t}^e = q_{i,t-1}$;
        1.2.4. END;
    1.3. Perception of direct rivals $(i \neq k)$: $\Lambda_{i,t} = \left(k : \left|x_{k,t} - x_{i,t}\right| \leq \sigma_i x_t^{max}\right)$;
    1.4. Set mark-up $\mu_{i,t} = \dfrac{\eta + \sum_{k \in \Lambda_{k,t-1}} s_{k,t-1}}{\eta + \sum_{k \in \Lambda_{k,t-1}} s_{k,t-1} - s_{i,t}^e}$, $s_{i,t}^e = \dfrac{1}{Card(S_t^1)}$ for new firms and $s_{i,t}^e = s_{i,t-1}$ otherwise;
    1.5. Pricing: $p_{i,t} = \mu_{i,t} c_{i,t}^e$;
    1.6. New knowledge at t: $\gamma_{i,t} \sim Dist.$, with "*Dist.*" a (truncated) Pareto distribution, supporting values $L = 0$, $H = 1$ and parameter θ (slope of density function). The lower the value of θ, the more probable it is that we get large knowledge improvements (large $\gamma_{i,t}$). We have θ in our model:

$$\theta = \frac{1}{\phi \cdot imitation + (1 - \phi) \cdot research};$$

$imitation = \frac{x_t^{max} - x_{i,t}}{x_{i,t}}$, that is, assimilation of knowledge from the gap to the frontier;

$research = \frac{R_{i,t}}{R_{i,t}^{max}}$, that is, knowledge obtained from inner R&D;

3. END;

➢ Define Operate_Sector2:

1. For each firm j:
    1.1. Re-scaling $X_{j,t-1}$ to be comparable with the values $x_{k,t}$; values $X_{j,t-1}$ range within $\left(0, \frac{1}{Card(S_t^1)-1}\right)$, whereas the values $x_{k,t}$ range in $\left(0, \frac{1}{Card(S_t^1)}\right)$ we have an additional firm in the current period:

$$X_{j,t-1}' = X_{j,t-1} \cdot \frac{Card(S_t^1) - 1}{Card(S_t^1)};$$

    1.2. Set of understandable machines: $\Xi_{j,t} = \left(k : \left|X_{j,t-1}' - x_{k,t}\right| \leq \rho_j x_t^{max}\right)$;
    1.3. Buy a machine from i with probability proportional to:

$$\alpha_1 x_{i,t} + (1 - \alpha_1) \left(1 - \frac{p_{i,t}}{\sum_{k \in \Xi_{j,t}} p_{k,t}} \right);$$

$$c_{j,t} = p_{i,t};$$

$$X_{j,t} = x_{i,t};$$

$$y_{j,t} = x_{i,t};$$

1.4. Pricing: $p_{j,t} = \left(\frac{\delta}{\delta - s_{j,t}} \right) c_{j,t}$

1.5. Firm j competitivenes in the consumption goods market:

$$f_{j,t} = \alpha_2 \frac{y_{j,t}}{y_t^{max}} + (1 - \alpha_2) \left(1 - \frac{p_{j,t}}{p_t^{max}} \right);$$

2. END;

➢ Define Apply_ Replicator_Sector1:

1. For each firm i in Sector 1, update performance by:

$$\frac{x_{i,t+1} - x_{i,t}}{x_{i,t}} = \gamma_{i,t} - \bar{\gamma}_t, \bar{\gamma}_t = \sum_k x_{k,t} \gamma_{k,t};$$

2. END;

➢ Define Apply_Replicator_Sector2:

1. For each j in Sector 2, calculate its market share from the replicator equation:

$$\frac{s_{j,t+1} - s_{j,t}}{s_{j,t}} = f_{j,t} - \bar{f}_t, \quad \bar{f}_t = \sum_h s_{h,t} f_{h,t};$$

2. END;

➢ Define Exit_Sector1:

1. For each firm i in Sector 1:

    1.1. Calculate ex post unit cost: $c_{i,t} = c + \frac{R_{i,t}}{q_{i,t}}$;

    1.2. Calculate profit: $\pi_{i,t} = q_{i,t} (p_{i,t} - c_{i,t})$;

    1.3. Firm i exists the market when $\pi_{i,t} \leq 0$;

    1.4. Normalize: . $\sum_i x_{i,t+1} = \sum_i x_{i,t} = 1$ Note that firm exit alters the relative values of technological levels in the sector.

    1.5. Communicate to Sector 2 the re-scaling in the previous step;

2. END;

➢ Define Exit_Sector2:

1. Each firm j in Sector 2 exists the market when: $s_{j,t+1} \leq 0.005$;
2. Normalize: $\sum_i s_{i,t+1} = 1$;
3. END;

Appendix B

Utopia Competition: Microfoundations for the Replicator Dynamics and the Formal Analysis for One Isolated Subsystem

B1 Microfoundations

Let us denote by f_{ij} the rate at which citizens contributing x_j switch to behavior x_i, in their pursuing of more satisfactory behavioral patterns. Let us consider that this switching rate is:

$$f_{ij} = \theta[u_i - u_j]_+ = \theta max(u_i - u_j; 0), \quad \theta > 0$$

where $\theta > 0$ captures the ease with which citizens may change their behavior. We are assuming that, given the payoff criteria in Section 5.2.1, when a citizen from behavioral group i meets another from j, they discover the possibility of adopting behavior x_j. We then propose that there exists a certain flow of citizens gradually moving in the "better-valuation" direction, instead of having a fully rational representative citizen.

Thus, assuming that the product $\delta s_i s_j (0 < \delta < 1)$ gives the probability for a random and independent interaction between one citizen with contribution i (share in the population s_i) and another with behavioral pattern j (share s_j), in a small interval Δt, the flow of citizens from j to i would be given by:

$$\delta s_i s_j f_{ij} \Delta t$$

and the change in the proportion of citizens with behavior x_i would be:

$$\Delta s_i = \sum_j \delta s_i s_j (f_{ij} - f_{ji}) \Delta t, \quad f_{ij} - f_{ji} = \theta(u_i - u_j).$$

Additionally, we consider that the agents may also choose their contribution randomly with a small probability μ, due to nonmodeled factors. If we add this component to the replicator equation above, we obtain the following replicator with random experimentation:

$$\Delta s_i = (1 - \mu) \sum_j \theta \delta s_i s_j (u_i - u_j) \Delta t + \mu \left(\frac{1}{n} - s_i\right) \Delta t$$

The term that accounts for random experimentation is composed of the outflow μs_i (which is proportional to the number of agents choosing contribution x_i) and the inflow $\frac{\mu}{n}$ (which, given that it is random decision, and there are n possible alternatives, is proportional to $\frac{1}{n}$). Thus, the net flow of agents changing their contribution from x_i to x_j because of random experimentation is $\frac{(s_j - s_i)}{n}$.

Therefore, the continuous time evolution of the proportion of citizens with contribution i may be described by the following equation (Fatas-Villafranca et al. 2011):

$$\frac{ds_i}{dt} = (1 - \mu)\sum_j \delta s_i s_j \left(f_{ij} - f_{ji} \right) + \mu \left(\frac{1}{n} - s_i \right)$$

$$= (1 - \mu)\delta s_i \sum_j s_j \theta (u_i - u_j) + \mu \left(\frac{1}{n} - s_i \right),$$

$$\dot{s}_i = (1 - \mu)\theta \delta s_i \left(u_i - \sum_j s_j u_j \right) + \mu \left(\frac{1}{n} - s_i \right)$$

or changing velocity ($i = 1, ..., n$):

$$\dot{s}_i = (1 - \mu)s_i(u_i - \bar{u}) + \mu \left(\frac{1}{n} - s_i \right), \quad \bar{u} = \sum_j s_j u_j.$$

In this way, we obtain the expressions in equation (2) in Section 5.2.2 and – through a similar reasoning – the system expressed in equation (3) in Section 5.2.3 for the relative share of subsystems in society.

Let us note that, if (for the sake of simplicity and without losing any generality) we consider the traditional case in which $\mu = 0$, then we obtain a typical replicator dynamics system with endogenously changing payoff levels such as the one that follows:

$$\dot{s}_i = s_i(u_i - \bar{u})$$

B2 A Formal Analysis for Intra-subsystem Dynamics

Let us consider the analysis of one subsystem in isolation, with the intra-subsystem structure being composed of three levels of citizen contribution:

$$x_1, \quad x_2 = (1 + a)x_1, \quad x_3 = (1 + a)x_2, \quad a > 0.$$

We consider this formal representation for intra-subsystem dispersion among behavioral patterns for mathematical simplicity. In Fatas-Villafranca, Saura and Vazquez (2009), we can see that the results are qualitatively similar to the ones obtained for an arithmetic progression among contribution levels of different citizens.

Considering equation (1) in Section 5 of this Element, we may rewrite this as follows:

$$u_i = \alpha x_i + \beta(s_{i+1} - s_{i-1})x_i, \quad \alpha, \beta \in (0,1), \quad (i = 1,2,3)$$

If we now combine this simplified expression with the replicator system without mutations

$$\dot{s}_i = s_i(u_i - \bar{u})$$

we can use both expressions and see that the intra-subsystem dynamics can be analyzed by exploring the following system:

$$
\begin{cases}
\dot{s}_1 = s_1(\alpha x_1 + \beta s_2 x_1 - \bar{u}) \\
\dot{s}_2 = s_2\left(\alpha x_2 + \beta(s_3 - s_1)x_2 - \bar{u}\right) \\
\dot{s}_3 = s_3(\alpha x_3 - \beta s_2 x_3 - \bar{u})
\end{cases}
\tag{B2-1}
$$

Given that the unit-simplex is not altered by the flows induced by equation (B2-1), the dynamics of equation (B2-1) are essentially driven by the plane system ($s_3 = 1 - s_1 - s_2$):

$$
\begin{cases}
\dot{s}_1 = s_1(\alpha x_1 + \beta s_2 x_1 - \hat{u}) \\
\dot{s}_2 = s_2\left(\alpha x_2 + \beta(1 - 2s_1 - s_2)x_2 - \hat{u}\right) \\
\hat{u} = s_1(\alpha x_1 + \beta s_2 x_1) + s_2[\alpha x_2 + \beta(1 - 2s_1 - s_2)x_2] \\
\quad + (1 - s_1 - s_2)(\alpha x_3 - \beta s_2 x_3).
\end{cases}
\tag{B2-2}
$$

In Fatas-Villafranca, Saura and Vazquez (2007) we analyzed a mathematical system that is formally identical to equation (B2-2). There we proved that what in our current case would be the intra-subsystem dynamics driven by equation (B2-2) depends on specific parametric conditions. More precisely, our intra-subsystem dynamics as stated in a simplified manner in equation (B2-2) are determined by the following parametric conditions:

1) If we set $\beta > \alpha a$, that is to say, when the influence of intra-subsystem local peer interactions (the local externalities) are sufficiently intense, then the interactions between citizens with distinct behavioral patterns within the same subsystem (utopia) will maintain the subsystem in an indefinite process of endogenous self-transformation. There will be an ongoing process of cycling flows of citizens updating and revising their behavior.

This is what in Fatas-Villafranca et al. (2007, 2009) we called a *dynamic diversity* D-Regime. This result is also relevant for our study in Section 5 in this Element. In fact, it is fully in line with the discussion that we have presented in terms of the subgames and their mixture.

2) On the contrary, when we have (or set up) the condition $\beta < \alpha a$, then we obtain a *conformity* C-Regime in which citizens tend to concentrate gradually on either one or two levels of citizenship. This means a concentration of citizen behavioral patterns as time goes by. For the sake of the analysis in Section 5, we take into account these results, which help us to understand the dynamics of the coevolutionary approach to political economy suggested in this Element.

References

Acemoglu, D. and Robinson, J. A. (2012). *Why Nations Fail: The Origins of Power, Prosperity and Poverty.* New York: Crown Publishing Group.

Adner, R. and Kapoor, R. (2010). Value creation in innovation ecosystems: How the structure of technological interdependence affects firm performance in new technology generations. *Strategic Management Journal,* 31(3), 306–333.

Aghion P. and Griffith, R. (2005). *Competition and Growth.* Cambridge, MA: MIT Press.

Aghion P. and Howitt, P. (1998). *Endogenous Growth Theory.* Cambridge, MA: *MIT Press.*

Agrawal, R. (2018). *Built: The Hidden Stories behind Our Structures.* London: Bloomsbury Publishing.

Almudi, I. and Fatas-Villafranca, F. (2018). Promotion and co-evolutionary dynamics in contemporary capitalism. *Journal of Economic Issues,* 52(1), 80–102.

Almudi, I., Fatas-Villafranca, F., Fernandez, C., Potts, J. and Vazquez, F. J. (2020). Absorptive capacity in a two-sector neo-Schumpeterian model: a new role for innovation policy. *Industrial and Corporate Change,* 29(2), 507–531.

Almudi, I., Fatas-Villafranca, F. and Izquierdo, L. R. (2012). Innovation, catch-up and leadership in science-based industries. *Industrial and Corporate Change,* 21(2), 345–375.

Almudi, I., Fatas-Villafranca, F. and Izquierdo, L. R. (2013). Industry dynamics, technological regimes and the role of demand. *Journal of Evolutionary Economics,* 23, 1073–1098.

Almudi, I., Fatas-Villafranca, F., Izquierdo, L. R. and Potts, J. (2017). The economics of utopia: A co-evolutionary model of ideas, citizenship and socio-political change. *Journal of Evolutionary Economics,* 27, 629–662.

Almudi, I., Fatas-Villafranca, F., Jarne, G. and Sanchez, J. (2020). An evolutionary growth model with banking activity. *Metroeconomica,* 71(2), 392–430.

Almudi, I., Fatas-Villafranca, F., Potts, J. and Thomas, S. (2018). Absorptive capacity of demand in sports innovation. *Economics of Innovation and New Technology,* 27(3), 1–15.

Almudi, I., Fatas-Villafranca, F. and Sanchez, J. (2016). A formal discussion of the Sarewitz-Nelson rules. *Economics of Innovation and New Technology,* 25, 714–730.

Arrow, K. J. (1962a). Economic welfare and the allocation of resources for invention. 609–626. In Richard R. Nelson (ed.), *The Rate and Direction of Inventive Activity*. Princeton: Princeton University Press.

Arrow, K. J. (1962b). The economic implications of learning by doing. *Review of Economic Studies*, 29(1), 155–173.

Bloch, H. and Metcalfe, J. S. (2018). Innovation, creative destruction and price theory. *Industrial and Corporate Change*, 27(1), 1–13.

Bush, V. (1945). *Science the Endless Frontier*. Washington, DC: US Government Printing Office.

Bushan, B. (2017). *Springer Handbook of Nanotechnology*. Berlin: *Springer*.

Camprubi, L. (2014). *Engineers and the Making of the Francoist Regime*. Cambridge, MA: MIT Press.

Cantner, U., Savin, I. and Vannuccini, S. (2019). Replicator dynamics in value chains: Explaining some puzzles of market selection. *Industrial and Corporate Change*, 28(3), 589–611.

Chai, A. and Baum, C. (eds.) (2019). *Demand, Complexity and Long-Run Economic Evolution*. Cham: Springer Nature.

Ciarli, T., Lorentz, A., Valente, M. and Savona, M. (2019). Structural changes and growth regimes. *Journal of Evolutionary Economics*, 29(1), 119–176.

Cohen, W. M. and Levinthal, D. A. (1990). Absorptive capacity: A new perspective on learning and innovation. *Administrative Science Quarterly*, 35(1), 128–152.

Davidson, S., De Filippi, P. and Potts, J. (2018). Blockchains and the economic institutions of capitalism. *Journal of Institutional Economics*, 14(4), 639–658.

Delli Gatti, D., Fagiolo, G., Gallegati, M., Richiardi, M. and Russo, A. (2018). *Agent-Based Models in Economics*. New York: *Cambridge University Press*.

Denzau, A. T. and North, D. C. (2000). Shared mental models: Ideologies and institutions. 23–46. In A. Lupia, M. McCubbins and S. L. Popkin (eds.), *Elements of Reason*. New York. Cambridge University Press.

Dewey, J. (1927). *The Public and Its Problems*. Athens, OH: Swallow Press.

Dollimore, D. and Hodgson, G. M. (2014). Four essays on economic evolution: An introduction. *Journal of Institutional Economics*, 24(1), 1–10.

Dopfer, K. (ed.) (2005). *The Evolutionary Foundations of Economics*. Cambridge: Cambridge University Press.

Dopfer K. and Potts, J. (2008). *The General Theory of Economic Evolution*. London: *Routledge*.

Dosi, G. and Orsenigo, L. (1988). Coordination and transformation: An overview of structures, behaviours and change in evolutionary environments. In

G. Dosi, C. Freeman, R. R. Nelson, G. Silverberg and L. Soete (eds.), *Technical Change and Economic Theory*, 13–37. London: Pinter.

Dosi,G., Fagiolo, G., Napoletano, M. and Roventini, A. (2013). Income distribution, credit and fiscal policies in an agent-based Keynesian model. *Journal of Economic Dynamics and Control*, 37(8), 1598–1625.

Dosi G., Freeman C., Nelson R. R., Silverberg G. and Soete L. (eds.) (1988). *Technical Change and Economic Theory*. London: Pinter.

Dosi, G. and Grazzi, M. (2010). On the nature of technologies. *Cambridge Journal of Economics*, 34(1), 173–184.

Dosi, G., Marengo L. and Fagiolo, G. (2005). Learning in evolutionary environments. In K. Dopfer (ed.), *The Evolutionary Foundations of Economics*, 255–338. Cambridge: Cambridge University Press.

Dosi, G. and Nelson, R. R. (2010). Technical change and industrial dynamics as an evolutionary processes. In B. H. Hall and N. Rosenberg (ed.), *Handbook of the Economics of Innovation*, 51–127. Amsterdam: Elsevier.

Dosi, G. and Nuvolari, A. (2020). Introduction: Chris Freeman's History, Coevolution and economic growth. An affectionate reappraisal. *Industrial and Corporate Change*, 29(4), 1021–1034.

Dosi, G., Pereira, M. and Virgillito, M. E. (2017). The footprint of evolutionary processes of learning and selection upon the statistical properties of industrial dynamics. *Industrial and Corporate Change*, 26(2), 187–210.

Dosi, G. and Roventini, A. (2019). More is different and complex! The case for agent-based macroeconomics. *Journal of Evolutionary Economics*, 29(1), 1–37.

Earl, P. and Potts, J. (2013). The creative instability hypothesis. *Journal of Cultural Economics*, 37(2), 153–173.

Earl, P. and Potts, J. (2016). The management of creative vision and the economics of creative cycles. *Management and Decision Economics*, 37(7), 474–484.

Fatas-Villafranca, F., Férnández-Márquez, C. M. and Vázquez, F. J. (2019). Consumer social learning and industrial dynamics. *Economics of Innovation and New Technology*, 28(2), 119–141.

Fatas-Villafranca, F., Jarne, G. and Sanchez, J. (2009). Industrial leadership in science-based industries: A co-evolution model. *Journal of Economic Behavior and Organization*, 72(1), 390–407.

Fatas-Villafranca, F., Jarne, G. and Sanchez, J. (2012). Innovation, cycles and growth. *Journal of Evolutionary Economics*, 22(2), 207–233.

Fatas-Villafranca, F., Jarne, G. and Sanchez, J. (2014). Stock and mobility of researchers and industrial leadership. *Metroeconomica*, 65(1), 95–122.

Fatas-Villafranca, F., Sanchez, J. and Jarne, G. (2008). Modeling the co-evolution of national industries and institutions. *Industrial and Corporate Change*, 17(1), 65–108.

Fatas-Villafranca, F., Saura, D. and Vazquez, F. J. (2007). Emulation, prevention and social interaction in consumption dynamics. *Metroeconomica*, 58 (4), 582–608.

Fatas-Villafranca, F., Saura, D. and Vazquez, F. J. (2009). Diversity, persistence and chaos in consumption patterns. *Journal of Bioeconomics*, 11(1), 43–63.

Fatas-Villafranca, F., Saura, D. and Vazquez, F. J. (2011). A dynamic model of public opinion formation. *Journal of Public Economic Theory*, 13(3), 417–441.

Fernández-Márquez, C. M., Fatas-Villafranca, F. and Vázquez, F. J. (2017a). Endogenous demand and demanding consumers: A computational approach. *Computational Economics*, 49(2), 307–323.

Fernández-Márquez, C. M., Fatas-Villafranca, F. and Vázquez, F. J. (2017b). A computational consumer-driven market model: statistical properties and the underlying industry dynamics. *Computational and Mathematical Organization Theory*, 23(3), 319–346.

Foray, D., David, P. and Hall, B. (2009). Smart specialization: The concept. In *Knowledge for Growth*. Brussels: European Commission.

Foster, J. and Metcalfe, J. S. (eds.) (2001). *Frontiers of Evolutionary Economics*. Cheltenham: *Edward Elgar*.

Freeman, C. (1987). *Technology Policy and Economic Performance: Lessons from Japan*. London: Pinter.

Freeman, C. (1988). Introduction. In G. Dosi, C. Freeman, R. R. Nelson, G. Silverberg and L. Soete (eds.), *Technical Change and Economic Theory*, 1–8. London: Pinter.

Gilboa, I. (ed.) (2004). *Uncertainty in Economic Theory*. London: Routledge.

Gordon, R. (2012). Is US economic growth over? Faltering innovation confronts the six headwinds. NBER Working Paper No. 18315.

Haldane, A. G. and Turrell, A. E. (2019). Drawing in different disciplines: Macroeconomic agent-based models. *Journal of Evolutionary Economics*, 29 (1), 39–66.

Hodgson, G. M. (2015). *Conceptualizing Capitalism*. Chicago. University of Chicago Press.

Hodgson, G. M. (2019). *Evolutionary Economics: Its Nature and Future*. Elements in Evolutionary Economics. Cambridge: Cambridge University Press.

Hodgson, G. M. and Knudsen, T. (2010). *Darwin's Conjecture*. Chicago: University of Chicago Press.

Hofbauer, J. and Sigmund, K. (1998). *Evolutionary Games and Population Dynamics*. Cambridge: Cambridge University Press.

Jacobides, M. G., Cennamo, C. and Gawer, A. (2018). Toward a theory of ecosystems. *Strategic Management Journal*, 39(8), 2255–2276.

Kahneman, D. (2003). Maps of bounded rationality: Psychology for behavioral economics. *American Economic Review*, 93, 1449–1475.

Lippmann, W. (1922). *Public Opinion*. New York: *Simon & Schuster.*

Lipsey, R. G. (2018). *A Reconsideration of the Theory of Non-linear Scale Effects*. Elements in Evolutionary Economics. Cambridge: Cambridge University Press.

Lundvall, B. A. (1992). *National Systems of Innovation: Toward a Theory of Innovation and Interactive Learning*. London: Pinter.

Luppia, A., McCubbins, M. and Popkin, S. (eds.) (2000). *Elements of Reason: Cognition, Choice and the Bounds of Rationality*. New York: Cambridge University Press.

Malerba, F., Edquist, C. and Steinmueller, E. (eds.) (2004). *Sectoral Systems of Innovation*. New York: Cambridge University Press.

Malerba, F., Nelson, R. R., Orsenigo, L. and Winter, S. G. (2016). *Innovation and the Evolution of Industries: History-Friendly Models*. Cambridge: Cambridge University Press.

Markey-Towler, B. (2016). Law of the jungle: Firm survival and price dynamics in evolutionary markets. *Journal of Evolutionary Economics*, 26(3), 655–696.

Markey-Towler, B. (2019). The competition and evolution of ideas in the market sphere: A new foundations for institutional theory. *Journal of Institutional Economics*, 15(1), 27–48.

Martin, S. and Scott, J. (2000). The nature of innovation market failure and the design of public support for private innovation. *Research Policy*, 29(4), 437–447.

Metcalfe, J. S. (1998). *Evolutionary Economics and Creative Destruction*. London: Routledge.

Metcalfe, J. S. (2010). Technology and economic theory. *Cambridge Journal of Economics*, 34(1), 153–171.

Metcalfe, J. S., Foster, J. and Ramlogan, R. (2006). Adaptive economic growth. *Cambridge Journal of Economics*, 30(1), 7–32.

Montgomery, S. and Chirot, D. (2015). *The Shape of the New*. Princeton: *Princeton University Press.*

Muñoz, F. F., Encinar, M. I. and Cañibano, C. (2011). On the role of intentionality in evolutionary economic change. *Structural Change and Economic Dynamics*, 22(3), 193–203.

Murmann, J. P. (2003). *Knowledge and Competitive Advantage: The Coevolution of Firms, Technology and National Institutions*. New York: Cambridge University Press.

Nelson, R. R. (1959). The simple economics of basic scientific research. *Journal of Political Economy*, 77, 297–306.

Nelson, R. R. (ed.) (1962). *The Rate and Direction of Inventive Activity*. Princeton: Princeton University Press.

Nelson, R. R. (1982). The role of knowledge in R&D efficiency. *Quarterly Journal of Economics*, 97(3), 453–470.

Nelson, R. R. (ed.) (1993). *National Innovation Systems*. Oxford: Oxford University Press.

Nelson, R. R. (1995). Recent evolutionary theorizing about economic change. *Journal of Economic Literature*, 33, 48–90.

Nelson, R. R. (1988). Institutions supporting technical change in the United States. In G. Dosi, C. Freeman, R. R. Nelson, G. Silverberg and L. Soete (eds.), *Technical Change and Economic Theory*, 312–239. London: Pinter.

Nelson, R. R. (2008). Economic development from the perspective of evolutionary economic theory. *Oxford Development Studies*, 36(1), 9–21.

Nelson, R. R. (2012). Some features of research by economists foreshadowed by "The Rate and Direction of Inventive Activity." In J. Lerner and S. Stern (eds.), *The Rate and Direction of Inventive Activity Revisited*, 35–42. Chicago: University of Chicago Press.

Nelson, R. R. (2018). *Modern Evolutionary Economics: An Overview*. New York: Cambridge University Press.

Nelson, R. R. and Sampat, B. (2001). Making sense of institutions as a factor shaping economic performance. *Journal of Economic Behavior and Organization*, 44(1), 31–54.

Nelson, R. R. and Winter, S. G. (1982). *An Evolutionary Theory of Economic Change*. Cambridge, MA: Harvard University Press.

North, D. C. (2005). *Understanding the Process of Economic Change*. Princeton: Princeton University Press.

Novak, M. (2018). *Inequality: An Entangled Political Economy Perspective*. London: Palgrave Macmillan.

Nowak, M. (2006). *Evolutionary Dynamics*. Cambridge, MA: Belknap Press.

Page, B. and Shapiro, R. Y. (1992). *The Rational Public*. Chicago: University of Chicago Press.

Potts, J. (2000). *The New Evolutionary Microeconomics*. Cheltenham: Edward Elgar.

Pretel, D. and Camprubi, L. (eds.) (2018). *Technology and Globalization*. Palgrave Studies in Economic History. London: Macmillan.

Pyka, A. (2017). Dedicated innovation systems to support the transformation towards sustainability. *Journal of Open Innovation: Technology, Market, Complexity*, 3(1), 27.

Pyrgidis, C. N. (2018). *Railway Transportation Systems: Design, Construction and Operation*. London: Taylor & Francis.

Rodrik, D. (2004). Industrial policy for the 21st century. Harvard University Working Paper No. RWP04-047.

Sandholm, W. (2010). *Population Games and Evolutionary Dynamics*. Cambridge, MA: MIT Press.

Sarewitz, D. and Nelson, R. R. (2008a). Three rules for technological fixes. *Nature*, 456, 871–872.

Sarewitz, D. and Nelson, R. R. (2008b). Progress in know-how: Its origins and limits. *Innovations: Technology, Governance, Globalization*, 3(1), 101–117.

Saviotti, P. P. and Pyka, A. (2004). Economic development by the creation of new sectors. *Journal of Evolutionary Economics*, 14(1), 1–35.

Saviotti, P. P. and Pyka, A. (2013). The coevolution of innovation, demand and growth. *Economics of Innovation and New Technology*, 22(5), 461–482.

Schumpeter, J. A. (1942). *Capitalism, Socialism and Democracy*. New York: Harper & Row.

Shapiro, R. Y. and Jacobs, L. R. (1989). The relationship between public opinion and public policy. In S. Long and (eds.), *Political Behavior Annual*, 1–50 . Boulder, CO: Westview.

Silverberg, G. and Soete, L. (eds.) (1994). *The Economics of Growth and Technical Change*. Aldershot: Edward Elgar.

Simon, H. (1955). A behavioural model of rational choice. *Quarterly Journal of Economics*, 69(1), 99–118.

Simon, H. (1957). *Models of Man*. New York: Wiley.

Simon, H. (1991). Bounded rationality and organizational learning. *Organization Science*, 2(1), 125–134.

Stachurski, J. (2016). *A Primer in Econometric Theory*. Cambridge, MA: MIT Press.

Stimson, J. A. (1991). *Public Opinion in America: Moods, Cycles and Swings*. Boulder, CO: Westview.

Trajtenberg, M. (2012). Can the Nelson-Arrow paradigm still be the beacon of innovation policy? In J. Lerner and S. Stern (eds.), *The Rate and Direction of Inventive Activity Revisited*, 679–684. Chicago: University of Chicago Press.

Trevelyan, J. (1992). *Robots for Shearing Sheep: Shear Magic*. Oxford: Oxford University Press.

Urmetzer, S., Schlaile, M., Bogner, K., Muller, M. and Pyka, A. (2018). Exploring the dedicated knowledge base of a transformation towards a sustainable bioeconomy. *Sustainability*, 10(6), 1694.

Van den Bergh, J., Savin, I. and Drews, S. (2019). Evolution of opinions in the growth-vs-environment debate: Extended replicator dynamics. *Futures*, 109, 84–100.

Vega-Redondo, F. (2007). *Complex Social Networks*. Cambridge: Cambridge University Press.

Weibull, J. W. (1995). *Evolutionary Game Theory*. Cambridge, MA: MIT Press.

Weidlich, W. (2006). *Sociodynamics: A Systematic Approach to Mathematical Modeling in the Social Sciences*. Mineola, NY: Dover Publications.

Wilson, D. S. and Kirman, A. (eds.) (2016). *Complexity and Evolution*. Cambridge, MA: MIT Press.

Winter, S. G. (1984). Schumpeterian competition in alternative technological regimes. *Journal of Economic Behavior and Organization*, 5(3), 287–320.

Winter, S. G. (2014). The future of evolutionary economics: Can we break out from the beach headed? *Journal of Institutional Economics*, 10(4), 613–644.

Witt, U. (2009). Novelty and the bounds of unknowledge in economics. *Journal of Economic Methodology*, 16(4), 361–375.

Witt, U. (2014). The future of evolutionary economics: Why the modalities of explanation matter? *Journal of Institutional Economics*, 10(4), 645–664.

Zadeh, L. A. (1965). Fuzzy sets. *Information and Control*, 8(1), 333–353.

Cambridge Elements ≡

Evolutionary Economics

John Foster
University of Queensland
John Foster is Emeritus Professor of Economics the University of Queensland, Brisbane. He is Fellow of the Academy of Social Science in Australia; Life member of Clare Hall College, Cambridge; and Past President of the International J.A. Schumpeter Society. He is also Director of the Energy Economics and Management Group at UQ and Focal Leader for Renewable Energy at the Global Change Institute.

Jason Potts
RMIT University
Jason Potts is Professor of Economics at RMIT University, Melbourne. He is also an Adjunct Fellow at the Institute of Public Affairs. His research interests include technological change, economics of innovation, and economics of cities. He was the winner of the 2000 International Joseph A. Schumpeter Prize and has published over 60 articles and six books.

About the Series
Elements in Evolutionary Economics provides comprehensive overviews of the major building blocks of evolutionary economics across micro, meso and macro domains of analysis. It extends from theories of evolutionary economic behavior, entrepreneurship and the innovating firm, and agent-based modelling, to processes of variation and selection in evolutionary competition, industrial dynamics, evolutionary economics of institutions, emergent complexity, and evolutionary macroeconomics.

Cambridge Elements ☰

Evolutionary Economics

Elements in the Series

A Reconsideration of the Theory of Non-Linear Scale Effects: The Sources of Varying Returns to, and Economics of, Scale
Richard G. Lipsey

Evolutionary Economics: Its Nature and Future
Geoffrey M. Hodgson

Coevolution in Economic Systems
Isabel Almudi and Francisco Fatas-Villafranca

A full series listing is available at: www.cambridge.org/EEVE

Printed in the United States
by Baker & Taylor Publisher Services